TUNNEL VISION

Tadhg de Brún

**MENTOR
BOOKS**

First Published in 2009 by

MENTOR BOOKS
43 Furze Road,
Sandyford Industrial Estate,
Dublin 18,
Republic of Ireland.

Tel: +353 1 295 2112 / 3   Fax: +353 1 295 2114
e-mail: admin@mentorbooks.ie
www.mentorbooks.ie

A catalogue record for this book is available from the British Library

ISBN: 978-1-84210-395-1

Cover Photograph courtesy of Sportsfile

Edited by: Treasa O'Mahony
Layout & Cover Design: Kathryn O'Sullivan

Printed in Ireland by ColourBooks Ltd.

1 3 5 7 9 10 8 6 4 2

Contents

Acknowledgements

I would like to thank Danny McCarthy of Mentor Books for trusting me with this project. From day one, he was always on hand to give his expert advice when it was needed. And there were many times when that advice was needed.

Treasa O'Mahony was my editor, and she brought order to what at times was chaos. I'm sure there were times when she wondered if I would ever get to the end.

A special thanks to my Floor Manager colleagues in RTÉ who indulged me for years because of my passion for sport.

Dedication

I would like to dedicate this book to John Crown and the oncology staff in the day-care centre in St. Vincent's Private Hospital, Dublin. Many of the seeds for this book were sown while I was in their wonderful care.

Prologue

First Train to Croke Park

Galway beat Cork in the 1956 All-Ireland Football Final by three points. Due to a polio scare in Cork that summer, the game was not played until October. The final score was Galway 2–13, Cork 3–7. I do not need to check a book of statistics for this information. It is embedded in my memory as if it happened yesterday.

It was my first ever All-Ireland Final and also my first visit to the nation's capital city. I was 10 years old. My father was a fanatical Galway supporter who hailed from Cornamona, a tiny village situated on the shores of Lough Corrib in the Connemara Gaeltacht. His beloved county had been starved of success for 18 years. This October Sunday would at last, he hoped, bring redemption. He had one ticket for the game. I would be carried over the turnstile and would sit on his knee. This was a landmark day for me. Up to then I had been brought to many Connacht Championship matches in Castlebar, Tuam and the old St Coman's Park in Roscommon, but this was the real deal. The All-Ireland Final meant one thing to me in those days, and that was listening to the voice of Mícheál O'Hehir as he described the events in far-off Croke Park. 1956 would change all that; I would be there and see it all first hand.

For my father, travelling to a final was an excursion that had to be carefully and meticulously planned. We were to travel by train to Dublin, which meant a very early start to the day. My father would not be content to travel on the later train going to Dublin – we had to be on the first one available. He had arranged with the nuns in the local Mercy convent, Castlerea, County Roscommon that we could attend their community Mass in the chapel, at the ungodly hour of 7 a.m. This would be followed by a hurried breakfast at home, as my father always insisted on being at the train station long before the Dublin-bound train was due to arrive. It was not that he was worried about there being a last-minute rush at the ticket desk – he always purchased the tickets for the journey on the day before. If my father needed to be at a particular location at a given time, he would arrive at that location half an hour before he had to be there.

I remember little of the Mass with the good nuns that morning. The excitement of the occasion got the better of me, and I fainted in that lovely chapel. There was concern that this might be something more serious, but I ate a hearty breakfast to prove I was just fine.

I recall that the journey to Dublin seemed endless, but I suspect that it was my eagerness to get to Croke Park that gave me this impression. As the train made its way in through the suburbs of the city, the seasoned travellers on board readied themselves for a special moment. The wall at the railway end of Croke Park was much lower in those days, and passengers were afforded a clear view of the hallowed ground as the train passed on its way to Pearse Street Station. Loud cheers echoed over the railway wall. Maroon and white flags were pushed out the windows, almost in defiance, as we passed what would be the scene of battle in a few hours' time. Croke Park was empty as we passed on that train. The gates would not be open to the public for some time yet. The flag-waving was a statement of intent by the fans, an announcement of their arrival in Dublin, a message that they were ready for the fray.

The train emptied its passengers at Westland Row where we boarded the No 3 bus which would take us to Clonliffe Road, a short walk away from the famous ground. Part of Croke Park was a building site for that final of 1956. The old stand was being demolished and making way for the new Hogan Stand. This new stand would be a state-of-the-art structure, which, when completed, would accommodate 16,000 people. Almost 40 years later, I watched it being dismantled to make way for the progress of the premium and corporate box.

We made our way to the appropriate turnstile and waited for the gate to open. Croke Park was eerily quiet when eventually we were admitted. We were there far too early, but that was my father's way. The ritual had to be followed. The sandwiches and flask of tea were carefully unwrapped, and I was told to eat well as that would be the last taste of food until the homeward journey on the train that evening.

The Atmosphere on Match Day

Looking around Croke Park on that first visit, I tried to take it all in. The Canal End, the famous Hill 16 and the tall Cusack Stand. The later trains were passing by the railway end, behind the Hill, and their occupants waved their flags out the windows, as our fellow-travellers had done earlier. This time, those who were now inside the ground waved their flags at the passing train. It was as if they were urging their fellow-countrymen and women to hurry to the ground to support the cause. My father pointed out the two narrow tunnels in the old Cusack Stand from which the two teams would emerge, and I wondered what it was like in those dressing rooms. What did those rooms look like? Apart from the teams, who else was in those dressing rooms? What was being said in those dark, cavernous spaces, far removed from the gaze of the crowd?

In Tuam, in Roscommon or in Castlebar, supporters could walk past the dressing rooms before a game or wait outside afterwards to catch a glimpse of the players as they emerged. This was different. The teams were hidden away under the stand until it was time to enter the field to be greeted by a huge roar from the supporters. I also wondered who told the teams when it was time to take the field, and how did they know who would come out first and at what time? The hordes of photographers fascinated me too as they scurried around before the game flashing their neon bulbs, and then took their places behind the goalposts for the duration of the match. As they snapped their pictures, I wondered which ones we would see in *The Irish Press* which my father would buy first thing the next morning.

A few minutes before the start of the game, my father pointed out a man in the distance in a small box. This was Mícheál O'Hehir, who was about to bring the story of the game to thousands of radio listeners all over Ireland. The nation would hang on his every word. There were no television cameras. They would make their first appearance six years later.

To my father's delight, and mine, Galway won that final and the game is best remembered for the displays given by 'the terrible twins', Frank Stockwell and Sean Purcell. Stockwell scored two goals and five points that day, a record for an All-Ireland Final, which stands to this day. True, Dublin's Jimmy Keaveney bettered that by a point in the 1977 Final, but the playing time for a final had been extended to 70 minutes by then. Both records stand the test of time today.

That 1956 final was a great final for me, principally because it was the first one. A few years later, I would get to know many of those who played in that game, Purcell, Kirwan and the great Paddy Harrington (father of Padraig Harrington), who was on the losing side that day.

There was one thing that I was absolutely certain of after that day, and that was the fact that I liked these big occasions. I was hooked on the drama, the excitement, and for some strange reason I was totally fascinated by the press photographers as they went about their business, snapping off the pictures that would, by some miracle, appear in the following day's newspapers. I wanted to be part of it all.

The RTÉ Advertisement

The years passed and after finishing school I spent some time working first as a piano player in a hotel and then a circuit court official in Sligo.

One day I spotted a most interesting ad in a national daily newspaper. RTÉ, only five years in existence at the time, were looking for applications from candidates for the posts of 'studio operators'. I had no idea what the jobs entailed but was curious enough to send off an application, though I had no intention of leaving Sligo.

Two interviews later, RTÉ invited me to commence training in January 1967. This was an opportunity which was too good to miss. Television was still in its infancy in Ireland back then, indeed it was still a novelty. Terry Wogan, Gay Byrne, Kathleen Watkins, Charles Mitchell, Mícheál O'Hehir, Maurice O'Doherty, Fred Cogley and Nuala Donnelly had all attained superstar status in those early years of RTÉ. Turning down the chance to work among these icons was something I could not contemplate, and I presented myself for training in Montrose on 4 January 1967.

There were three areas of employment we trainees were to be assigned to – sound, lighting and cameras – depending on our suitability. For whatever reason I was sent to the camera department and was now officially designated as a trainee cameraman, with a take-home pay of seven pounds and one penny per week for the first six months. It was new, it was exciting, and we all wanted to be part of the great adventure. Nowadays, whenever I show some friends around the studios, I am always struck by the fact that they love to sit in the newsreader's chair to have their picture taken. Looking back, that is exactly what we rookies did in our early days when we got our first glimpses of the same studios. We couldn't wait to see programmes being recorded, or transmitted live, such was our enthusiasm to get involved in our new venture. But we would have to wait.

In those days, when RTÉ told you that you were to embark on a training course, that is exactly what it meant. Training, lots of it, and nothing else. Before the station opened a few years earlier, senior camera and lighting people from the BBC had joined up to recruit and train the new staff.

We were known as 'coolies', and that is what we were, doing the donkey work for the crew, rigging the cameras in the morning before rehearsal and hauling around the camera cables behind each individual camera. The senior cameraman taught us how to frame a shot properly and lectured us about the composition of various shots. For us, the coffee break could not come quickly enough, as that was our opportunity to have a go at operating those cumbersome cameras when the crew was on a break. We stayed in the studios during meal breaks in order to have a little more time putting into practice what we were being taught, such was our enthusiasm. Learning to operate a television camera is very much like learning to ride a bike – it's all about co-ordination. Once the operator has mastered the art of moving this machine around the studio, the next step of framing a shot and keeping it in focus becomes the priority. It was nerve-wracking having that senior cameraman standing behind us, watching our every move, as we pushed those monsters around the studio, lost focus and framing and stood on the cable by mistake. But slowly we began to get to grips with it.

I was in awe of those guys. They were good teachers and they were patient with us. But most of all, they were meticulous in everything they did in those studios. They were also determined that they would turn us into professional cameramen by the time our training came to an end.

In the meantime, we did what we were told and at all costs avoided incurring the wrath of the floor manager who ran the studio with an iron fist. RTÉ followed in the footsteps of the BBC when putting into place the structures for the running of a studio. The 'Beeb' was the best in the world, and probably still is. Its studio discipline was the blueprint for the way in which RTÉ would do things. It was important, therefore, to keep one's head down and not to attract the attention of the floor manager too much. After six months, our training came to an end. We lost the dubious honour of being 'coolies'. RTÉ made us permanent members of staff, and to my great relief, my salary doubled which removed me from the penury of those days in training. It was a superb training and sadly not the kind of training newcomers are given when they join the ranks of the studio crews today.

Television is a team business, and our training gave us a great grounding in the world of programme-making. Cutting corners was totally unacceptable. No matter how long it took, the job would not be finished until it was finished properly.

My early days as a fully-fledged cameraman were rather uninspiring to say the least. The 'rookies' were always despatched to Studio 3, which was the studio from which all news bulletins were transmitted. The camera movement was limited, but it was an ideal studio in which to overcome the fear of moving your camera 'on air', knowing that the shot in your viewfinder was the shot which was appearing in living rooms all over the country.

That Studio 3 was a grind, but we were eventually considered to be up to the challenge of facing bigger programmes, and better still, going out on location. I used to watch, with envy, as the large trucks, emblazoned with the 'Radio Telefís Éireann' logo, headed off for some part of the country.

Nowadays, when the RTÉ outside broadcast trucks roll into a town round the country, nobody pays any great attention. Back in those early days of television in Ireland, such a visit would cause huge excitement in the area and would be covered extensively by all the local papers. Not only were the 'stars' given a truly royal welcome, the crew too was feted on their arrival. None more so than the camera crew who had the power to ensure that people would be seen on TV, which was a huge novelty then.

Working on live broadcasts appealed to me most of all. There was a great air of excitement knowing that the audience at home were watching the picture in my viewfinder, as the action took place in front

of the camera. Sport provided the ideal opportunity for this, and in 1968, I made my Croke Park debut behind camera three in the old Hogan Stand tunnel. It was 12 years since my first visit to the venue.

1

The Irish Snooker Masters

RTÉ and the Irish Snooker Masters

The 1970s and 1980s were the halcyon days of snooker coverage on television. Prior to that, the game was perceived to be one which was played in dark, smoky rooms and had a shady aura to it. But television changed all that.

It brought the game to a whole new audience – in their living rooms. It was an easy game to follow for this new armchair viewer. Many of these new viewers remarked that watching snooker on television had a rather soothing effect. The arrival of colour television in the mid 1970s brought more dramatic change for the armchair viewer. There was now no need for commentators to utter the memorable line, 'for those of you watching in black and white, the pink ball is the one beside the blue!'

The game then had many great characters, all of whom in their own way attracted an even bigger audience. John Virgo, Willie Thorne, Steve Davis, Ray Reardon and Jimmy White were fast becoming household names. Virgo, perhaps, became the first snooker 'personality' away from the table by appearing on TV gameshows. Big Bill Werbeniuk came from Canada and his 20 stones in weight were matched only by the 20 pints of lager he drank during a match. An erratic but brilliant Alex Higgins mesmerised viewers not just with the quality of the snooker he played, but with his flamboyance off the table. I once talked to Steve Davis in the bowels of Goff's auditorium about the television mass coverage in the 1970s. Steve suggested it was '*Dallas* with balls!' It was very much a tongue-in-cheek description, but I knew what he meant.

Snooker was a different game back in those early television years. It was a slower, more ponderous game. Players were every bit as skilled as the present generation. But matches were slower, and it was not unusual for matches to go on into the early hours of the morning. One match, which involved the legendary Terry Griffiths, ended at 4 a.m.! The most famous late-night finish was, of course, the 1985 World Championship Final between Steve Davis and Dennis Taylor. Taylor, 8–0 down at one point, clawed his way back into the match to bring it to a final-frame decider. That last frame has now gone into snooker folklore with Taylor winning on the final black in front of a staggering 18.6 million television viewers. There have been many great finals since, but that 1985 final was undoubtedly the high point of snooker television coverage.

Interest in snooker has declined since those heady days of the 1970s and 1980s. Television coverage brought the game to the peaks of its popularity in those two decades. Ironically, it was overexposure on television that probably brought about the decline in its popularity. But the game still attracts a strong following, and there's a new generation of superstars on the block now. Stephen Hendry has surpassed Steve Davis's record of six world championships. Ronnie O'Sullivan is now regarded as the greatest player ever to take a cue in his hand. He's the new generation, and he's unpredictable but hugely talented.

Alex Higgins won the world championship in 1972 and, not surprisingly, his victory created a huge interest in the game in Ireland. Higgins attracted a massive following and was known as 'the people's champion'. Snooker clubs were not a feature in Ireland in those days and full-size snooker tables were usually to be found only in golf clubs or private clubs. The arrival of mass television coverage would change all that.

The first Irish Masters was broadcast by RTÉ in 1978 and was held in the National Stadium, the home of Irish boxing. It was not the ideal venue, but it was the start of a tournament which would run for 25 years. It found a new home at Goff's in County Kildare, a venue which was one of the best snooker venues in the world. This is not just my opinion but the view of all the top players in the world who played in the Benson & Hedges Irish Masters over a 20-year period.

Goff's – A Dream Arena

The first advantage Goff's had as a snooker venue was that it was a single-table venue. There simply was not enough room in the arena for a second table and this proved to be a godsend from a spectator perspective. Many tournaments played in Britain were played in a two-table arena up to the semi-final stage, but the Masters in Goff's was a single-table event for the full week. This was an added bonus from a TV point of view. There was no requirement to split the coverage over two tables which kept life much simpler.

Because of the pace of the game, television coverage of snooker is a simple and uncomplicated business. Two cameras on the floor of the arena, one to the left of the table, one to the right, covered the action looking up towards the baulk end. Two cameras on a raised platform covered the remainder of the action. One of these cameras is what we call 'a locked-off camera', that is an unmanned camera with a permanent wide-shot of the full table. The other is manually operated and follows the action from above as it unfolds around the table. Other cameras can be added to the coverage, such as cameras in the table pockets. These cameras, in my view, are just gimmicks and add little to the coverage.

The other great advantage that Goff's had as a snooker venue was that it was 'in the round'. The table was surrounded by the spectators, with the only gap being the area which housed the commentary box and the camera tower. This gave it a wonderful amphitheatre effect. The arena had a capacity for just under 1,000 people and on a packed night the atmosphere was electric. I have spoken to all the great players down through the years, and they agree on one thing. After the Crucible Theatre in Sheffield, home of the world championships, Goff's is the second-best snooker venue in the world. I have been to the Crucible, and there is no doubt it is indeed a very special venue. But it should be remembered that the Crucible is a theatre in the real sense, whereas Goff's is a building which was originally designed for selling horses. Its transformation into a world-class snooker venue for one week every year was remarkable.

Apart from the playing arena, it had many other distinct advantages. It had a spacious audience reception area, lots of bar and dining facilities and, very importantly, large car-parking areas. The top floor housed the players' bar, dining area for guests and the holy of holies, the office of Tournament Director Kevin Norton. Kevin ran a tight ship at the Masters every year. He built up a great team around him and he didn't suffer fools gladly. With Kevin, what you saw was what you got. While you might not always like it, you knew exactly where you stood. He was a professional who ran a great tournament, and the players loved him. Kevin had one other great attribute: he had a sense of humour, which came to his rescue on more than one occasion down through the years!

For those of us who worked on the tournament every year, our home for the week was a long corridor situated in the bowels of the building. This corridor led directly into the playing arena. It was a long, sprawling, semi-circular warren of rooms which housed some key personnel. The two rooms nearest to the arena were the players' dressing rooms. Next along the corridor was the room reserved for the match referees. Further down the corridor was the press room, a small, cramped area which housed the reporters from our own national dailies, members of the visiting British press and radio reporters from national and local stations. Shay Keenan was the Press Liaison Officer for the event and he presided over all matters relating to the media.

The referees' room was a very special place. For many years the two main referees at the Masters were John Street and John Williams. In latter years they were joined by Jaan Verhaas, the very affable Colin

Bryndad, Arien Williams (a retired policeman) and Paul Collier. Street and Williams were legendary. They were part of the snooker world for years and were as instantly recognisable as the players. John Williams often referred to himself as a 'leg end' as opposed to a legend. Between matches, or at mid-session breaks, he would regale us with the most inane and banal questions, none of which had an answer. Here's a sample of some of the best (or worst) ones.

Why is there only one monopolies commission?

How does the man who drives the snow-plough get to work?

Who put up the sign 'don't walk on the grass'?

That gives you a flavour of how we passed the time in the referees' room. I think you'll agree, it wasn't time well spent! There were also quiz questions, some genuine, some trick questions and, occasionally, some historical questions. Then there were the questions based on snooker – my favourite ones. Street and Williams would sneer at us in derision as we struggled to come up with answers. Some of these questions were genuine and based on situations they both had encountered in a lifetime involved in snooker. Here is a scenario which Williams came across at a match in England many years ago.

A player comes to the table, pots a red, fails to score with his next shot, and goes on to make a break of over one hundred. This is not a trick question. John Williams left us for a full day before he explained it to us. I'll let you mull over this for a while. Of course if you want to know the answer immediately, you can flick to page 197.

Dennis Taylor and the Collapsing Chair

There were many funny moments in the corridor just outside the playing arena. One such incident involved Dennis Taylor, Kevin Norton and a walkie-talkie. It was a Saturday afternoon and Taylor was involved in a semi-final against John Parrott, which was being broadcast live on television. For two frames, Taylor could do no wrong and was 2–0 up before John had settled in his chair. In the third frame, Taylor was at the table but, inexplicably, missed a 'sitter' of a red to let Parrott back in.

Taylor, disgusted with himself, walked away from the table and threw himself, literally, into his seat. Then something happened that I had never seen happen before. It was 'a first' for live snooker coverage on television. Taylor's chair collapsed from underneath him and he went sprawling onto the floor, with his jug of water and glass. His table, which was attached to the chair, also came crashing down, much to the merriment of the packed auditorium. The audience broke into whoops of laughter. Parrott, who was never slow to miss out on a bit of fun, came over to inspect the damage and quipped, 'Good job it wasn't Bill Werbeniuk!' (the portly 20-stone Canadian player).

John Street, who was refereeing the match, went over to have a look and, with help from Parrott and Taylor, tried to repair the damage sufficiently to get to the mid-session interval without further interruption. When order was restored, Parrott went on to win the remaining two frames and the players left the arena for the break. As they left, Taylor came to me in the corridor and asked me if I had a walkie-talkie with which he could communicate with Kevin Norton, Tournament Director. I told him I had, and asked him why he needed it. With a mischievous glint in his eye, he said 'I just want to have a little fun'. So we went into his dressing room and I showed Dennis how to use the walkie-talkie, and off he went.

'Dennis Taylor here calling Kevin Norton. Come in please, Kevin.'

'Yeah, Kevin here, Dennis. Whatcha want?'

'Kevin, I just want to let you know that I won't be going back out for the second session unless I get a guarantee that the chair I'm sitting on won't collapse from underneath me. It's a total disgrace that in a highly prestigious tournament like this a player can't be sure that his chair won't fall apart in the middle of the match.'

Norton, never a man to mince his words, realised instantly that he was being wound up and, after a very brief pause shot back:

'Dennis, if you spent more time on the table then you wouldn't have to worry about the fuckin' chair!'

I always remember the look on Dennis Taylor's face as he heard those words over the walkie-talkie; it was that look which said, 'What do I say now?' I just said to him, 'Game, set and match Dennis, forget it!'

For me, that was one of the great moments in Goff's and it was a testament to the respect the players had for Kevin Norton that he knew he could get away with such an audacious response. However, Taylor got his revenge not so long after!

Mike Hallett – Insult added to Injury

RTÉ broadcast another snooker tournament in the 1980s – a tournament which is largely forgotten now. It was known as the 'Carlsberg Challenge' and was actually played in the studios in Donnybrook. Studio 4 had just been built and was ideal for a one-table event. However, it had one drawback. It had no facility for a commentary box. To overcome this problem, a garden shed was put up on a gantry overlooking the studio floor and the late John Skehan, with that wonderful voice, did the match commentaries from this elevated piece of luxury which came from Woodies or some other DIY establishment.

The Carlsberg Challenge was specifically a television event and the top players were there by invitation. It was a very intimate kind of tournament – all activities took place in a very confined space. The press room was a large chorus room upstairs from the studio, which would later be used by bands appearing on *The Late Late Show*. The players' lounge was an audience waiting-area, and players' dressing rooms were the same ones used by Gay Byrne and his guests. The event had a pleasant family air to it, and everyone got to know one another. I got to know many of the players quite well during that event and I'm certain this helped greatly a few years later when I was confronted by a very awkward situation at the Masters in Goff's.

It happened on the Saturday night during the second semi-final between Ken Doherty and Mike Hallett. It was broadcast live at 7 p.m. Ken came out of the blocks flying and was 4–0 up in the blink of an eye. Hallett had barely got his hand on the table and, barring a major comeback, would miss out on a place in the final the next day. Not surprisingly, he was up against a totally partisan crowd who cheered every shot of Ken's to the rafters. Hallett was shell-shocked as Ken won the last frame before the mid-session break. He would become more shell-shocked as he left the arena for the calm of his dressing room. As Hallett walked out into the tunnel corridor, an RTÉ employee put his arm round his shoulder and grinned, 'Thanks very much Mike for the early night!'

Hallett was dumbfounded. I was directly behind him when the remark was passed, and I couldn't believe what I was hearing. Snooker was Hallett's profession. Now here he was being hammered in a hostile environment and being 'thanked' for letting people go home early. I followed him into the dressing room and apologised profusely for what happened. His manager had come down from the players' bar to give him a boost during the break and was told about what had happened in the tunnel. Not surprisingly, he was incensed and sent for Kevin Norton.

Hallett's manager wanted to make an official complaint about the incident. I pointed out that there was nothing I could do about it on the spot as the match was due to resume in a matter of minutes. Max Mulvihill, RTÉ Executive Producer, was now in Hallett's dressing room and he assured Hallett that the matter would be dealt with. Mike was very gracious that night and asked that the matter be dropped. He went back into the arena, won two frames, but lost the match 6–2. The incident has gone into Goff's folklore. Hallett doesn't play on the circuit

It looks as if Tadhg wants to take the snooker trophy
from Stephen Hendry at the Irish Snooker Masters!

Tadhg deep in conversation with Ms Jean Kennedy Smith,
US Ambassador to Ireland 1993 to 1998.

Goffs Arena, Co Kildare: Tadhg and snooker referee 'leg-end' John Williams
who had always wanted to be a TV cameraman.

Exterior view of the outside broadcasting unit. After a live transmission,
it folds up to become a truck again and heads for the next venue.

Tadhg and Marty Morrissey prepare for an interview
with Páraic Duffy, Director General of the GAA.

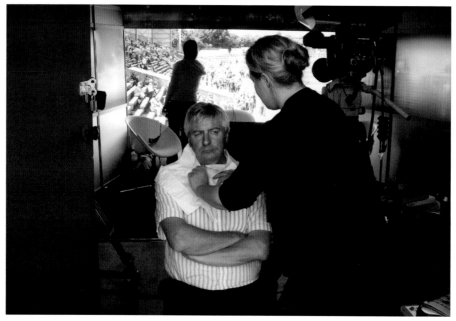

A less-than-ecstatic looking Micheal Lyster getting the
final touches to his make-up!

The bank of TV screens in the outside broadcasting unit.

The commentary box and presentation area in the splendid new
Shamrock Rovers ground in Tallaght. Building was still in progress
when RTÉ transmitted its first live game from the venue.

Martin Carney caught changing into his official RTÉ Sport
shirt on the Mayo minors' team bus!

The new studio in Thomond Park. The rugby panel of Tom McGurk, Brent Pope and Conor O'Shea – George Hook is on the way!

The post-match interview area in Thomond Park. All TV interviews must be conducted in front of the sponsor's backdrop.

Giovanni Trapattoni, Republic of Ireland soccer manager, faces the media glare at Croke Park during the qualification campaign for the 2010 World Cup in South Africa.

Ol' Blue Eyes was less forthcoming than Bob Hope when it came
to signing autographs. A burly security man put a quick stop
to any attempts by eager fans to have a chat.

The Holiday Inn, Tadhg's LA hotel, complete with view of
white igloos housing the local drug addict population.

The three amigos before the Three Tenors concert at Dodger Stadium, Los Angeles. Tadhg, George Hamilton and Maurice Reidy.

Mingling with the great and the good: At the Three Tenors' concert Bob Hope was happy to chat about Ireland, and Galway in particular. He had returned from there just a few days earlier.

Tadhg pictured here outside the famous Texas Book Depository on Dealey Plaza, Dallas from where Lee Harvey Oswald shot President John F Kennedy in 1963.

A copy of Tadhg's $1,000 tickets for the Three Tenors.
Even the tickets arrived by limousine!

The Cotton Bowl located in the historic Fair Park district of Dallas played host to the quarter-final between Brazil and Holland in USA 94.

Brazil versus Italy: World Cup final in Pasadena, California. George and Tadhg in the commentary box having escaped from the cab driver and the cockatoo.

The Brazilians, with Pele, were directly behind us on a few occasions.
There were more 'minders' than commentators.

Republic of Ireland defenders Steve Staunton and Kevin Moran make their
way to the team bus before their match against Italy. The Irish supporters
at the match outnumbered the Italians by nine to one!

Tadhg takes his place in the commentary box in RFK Stadium, Washington.
A large supply of liquid was essential in the summer heat.

George Hamilton gets ready to conduct his shortest interview ever with
Jack Charlton prior to Ireland's match against Italy.

The calm before the storm. The commentary booths in the Giants Stadium,
New Jersey. Not the most spacious or quiet of places! Brian Moore,
ITV's commentator, is pictured here taking a breather.

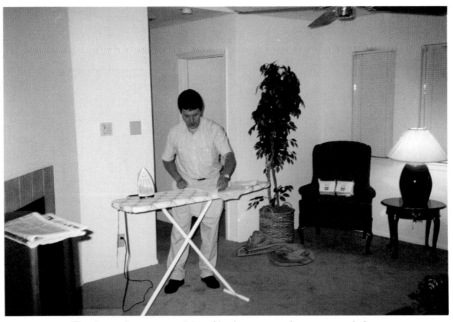

The less glamorous side of being a sports commentator:
George Hamilton irons his shirt in Dallas.

The closing ceremony of World Cup 94 held in the Rose Bowl, Pasadena, California was impressive. Note the cardboard boxes in the photo. At an earlier game in the tournament one of these boxes ended up around George Hamilton's head in a futile attempt to provide some shade from the searing heat of the sun.

Pat Hickey (Irish Olympic Council), Jack Charlton, Bill O'Herlihy
and Tadhg nervously await the outcome of the live draw
to see who Ireland will face in World Cup USA 94.

Despite Jack's relieved expression, Ireland ended up in a 'Group of Death'!
This group included Italy, Mexico and Norway. Tadhg looks apprehensive
while Michael Carruth (far left) and Pat Hickey don't look
too impressed with the draw!

anymore. He is now a very good commentator on television and, occasionally, when I hear his voice, I shudder slightly and think back to the night of his semi-final against Ken Doherty.

Alex Higgins – the Taylor Handshake & the Enigma

There were other tense nights in Goff's, none more so than the night Alex Higgins played Dennis Taylor. The trouble started a week earlier at a tournament in England, where an altercation had taken place between the two players. The fallout from all of this was that Higgins threatened to have Taylor shot the next time he went home to Northern Ireland. Inevitably, the incident made banner headlines and was an advertising bonanza for the meeting of the two the following week. There wasn't even standing room in the arena that night. The atmosphere was charged with emotion and people speculated wildly about the possibilities the night might bring. Rumours abounded, each more mad-cap than the other.

Down in the tunnel where the players were waiting to be introduced, the tension was palpable. Higgins, who had apologised to Taylor through the media, was trying to make small talk to Taylor and anyone else who cared to listen. Taylor was having none of it. It was clear to see that he was totally focused on this match – a match he was determined to win. For Dennis this was more than a snooker match. The noise level in the arena when the players were introduced was ear-splitting. Higgins was still the self-proclaimed 'people's champion' and still had a large following in the crowd, but it was clear after Taylor's introduction that the greater support was with him.

With the pre-match photographs out of the way, we reached the moment that people had wondered about all week: the handshake, or more importantly, would there be a handshake? Higgins saw the handshake as a further extension to his earlier apology, but Taylor saw it as nothing more than part of the usual pre-match ritual. His body language during the brief handshake said it all. He turned away from Higgins, looked at nobody in particular and went to his chair. Taylor made sure there was no eye-contact between Higgins and himself.

The match itself was an anti-climax which, considering what had gone on before it, was not surprising. Taylor won it comfortably. As he left the arena, there was a barely-concealed smile of quiet satisfaction on his face.

This was not the only time that Higgins caused a stir of excitement at the Irish Masters. He brought that excitement with him wherever he went, but 1989 would prove to be a special year for him at the Kildare venue. Just a week prior to the start of the event, Higgins was involved in an accident and sustained an injury to his ankle which left him limping badly. Nevertheless by the time Sunday came around, he was in the final. In a way, it was heroic, and yet comical, to watch him hobble around the table, sometimes jumping on one foot as he went on to become the first Irishman to win the event. The rapturous crowd bellowed out their support for the Belfastman, and the roars of approval which greeted his victory could be heard in nearby Naas. It was an amazing night of sport and of raw courage over adversity.

Later on that night I got an amazing insight into Higgins' snooker brain. Michael Lyster, who presented the programme that night on RTÉ, and myself were upstairs in the players' bar. We were the only people present in the bar as all the guests had gone on to the post-tournament reception in the City West Hotel. We stayed on to watch the highlights of Higgins's victory which was now being shown on television. Michael and I were taken aback a few minutes later when we found ourselves being joined by none other than Higgins himself. He had had ample time to celebrate his victory, but he was not in celebratory mood. In fact, he was looking for someone from the sponsors to give him his winning cheque. We assured him that his winnings would get to him in due course and suggested that he might like to savour his victory which was now being shown on the television in the room.

What followed was amazing. Higgins gave us a running commentary on the frame, shot by shot, and in many cases was ahead of the play. He explained to us what he had in mind when playing a particular shot, and where he wanted to get to, one or two shots later. He was able to take us through a break ahead of the action on the television and never called it wrong once. Then, just as quickly as he arrived, he was gone into the night. To say we were impressed would be a huge understatement. He was erratic, but he was a genius.

Taylor's Revenge

I mentioned earlier that Kevin Norton paid dearly for his great one-line put-down of Dennis Taylor, and he did. This is what happened.

It is customary when big sporting events are being televised that at some stage during the course of the week, the chief executive of the sponsor or the event director will be interviewed. This happened on major sports occasions such as the Irish Open golf, the Galway Races or Derby Day at The Curragh. The Irish Masters in Goff's was no different, and we had arranged to interview Kevin Norton at 2 p.m. on Sunday, before the start of the final. This interview would then be transmitted later in the day, usually at the mid-session break.

The tone of the interview was very general. It was a look back at the week's events, how it had all gone and 'are you generally happy with the way the week has unfolded'. There were no 'banana-skin' questions. Many of Norton's staff knew about the impending interview, and the night before there was a lot of banter about who should do his make-up and where he might get his hair specially done for the occasion. Norton took it all in good spirit but deep down he was a little nervous about the impending interview. He had good reason to be, because a plot was being hatched in the players' bar.

On the Saturday evening, Dennis Taylor came to me.

'I hear you're doing an interview with Kevin Norton tomorrow?' he asked.

'Yes Dennis, we are, in the auditorium at 2 p.m.,' I replied.

'Well Terry Griffiths and myself would like to be part of that interview, if you could set it up,' Taylor suggested, with an evil glint in his eye. Terry is a former world champion, and he was part of the commentary team at that time.

It was obvious we were into 'wind-up territory' here, and that this was payback time for the walkie-talkie put-down. John O'Brien was the producer who would be involved the next day and I laid out the scenario for him. He didn't need any convincing and saw immediately the potential for a lot of fun with the interview. Ronan Collins, who was to conduct the interview, was then brought on board. Ronan was exactly the man for the job and would know how to pitch it. No one else knew about the plans for the 'interview'.

Just before 2 p.m. on Sunday we all gathered in the still empty auditorium, with our three 'interviewees' sitting in the front row of the audience seats. The sound crew clipped on radio microphones, lights were checked and everything was conducted in a totally business-like manner. The interview was 'open ended', which meant there was no time restraint on it. I remember John O'Brien saying, 'We keep going no matter what happens'.

Ronan started by introducing everybody and asked Kevin was he happy with the way the week had gone. Kevin replied that it had been a great week with great snooker, and that the entire event had passed off without a glitch. Then Ronan asked Kevin why it was that the players enjoyed this tournament so much. Kevin, who was into his stride by now, explained that the players had only to worry about one thing when they came to Ireland – and that was playing snooker. All their other needs were taken care of by the organisers and the sponsors, and that he took great pride in running such a good event.

Then Ronan turned to Dennis Taylor, who agreed totally with what Kevin had said, and spoke on behalf of all the players when he said what a wonderful week the Irish Masters is. Griffiths reiterated what Taylor had said and spoke in glowing terms about the event. Ronan then said to Kevin Norton that it was remarkable how this tournament was trouble free down through the years. Kevin agreed and pointed out that any problems that arose were dealt with immediately, and people got on with the business of running the tournament. It was at this point that Griffiths lobbed in the hand-grenade.

'Except for the year with the Canadians, if you remember?' he said, to no one in particular.

This was a reference to a minor altercation which had taken place a few years earlier when Kirk Stephens, a new superstar from Canada, had turned up late for the start of his match.

Norton was taken aback by this and paled visibly. This was not the direction the interview was meant to be taking but he passed off the incident as a minor detail and one which was dealt with without any great fuss. But Taylor, sensing the moment, put on the pressure.

'But wasn't the Canadian Ambassador involved at the time?' Taylor piped up.

By now, the blood had drained from Kevin Norton's face as he battled, bravely, to pass the whole thing off as a storm in a teacup. Then Griffiths went for the jugular.

'If I remember rightly Kevin, you called one of them an arse-hole,' was his final contribution to the interview.

At that point Ronan stepped in and brought the whole thing to an end. Taylor and Griffiths walked away, delighted with their contribution, and Kevin Norton picked himself up off the floor of the auditorium, a shattered man. It was a few short minutes of madness and utter hilarity, which was enjoyed by all, except Kevin Norton. What we didn't know at the time, and to make matters worse, everyone in the players' bar was watching the 'interview' on closed-circuit television. To his credit, Kevin took it in his stride and admitted that it was a 'fair cop'. We did get around to recording the real interview eventually.

New Venue & Decline of the Masters

When new laws were introduced banning cigarette advertising on television, Benson & Hedges were forced to withdraw from sponsorship of the Masters. The tournament was now co-sponsored by the Department of Health and the City West Hotel and moved from its spiritual home in Goff's to City West. It was ironic that the message now from the sponsors was a strictly anti-smoking one. The new venue never had the charm or the atmosphere of the Kildare venue, and a lot of the fun went out of the event. However, the snooker tournament still had to be covered. For me, it was a labour of love because I happen to love the game of snooker. It gave me the opportunity to watch the best players in the world, close up. And yet I still managed to miss the John Higgins maximum break. I had slipped out of the arena for some reason and realised very quickly that the 147 was a possibility. However, I hadn't the nerve to sneak in the door in case I distracted Higgins. And there I stayed, while 30 feet away on the other side of the door, a maximum break was being made and I watched it on a screen.

While City West could never match Goff's as a snooker venue, the hotel and conference centre is a fine venue and has all the amenities required for hosting large numbers of people. The table was situated in the centre of the conference centre and 'bleachers' were erected on three sides of the table, which accommodated almost 2,000 people. There were gaps between the rows of seating and this meant that the amphitheatre effect, which was such a defining feature at Goff's, was missing at City West.

While I'm on the subject of seating accommodation for the public (or 'bleachers' as they are known in the television world) it is interesting to note how they got their name. The term 'bleachers' comes from American baseball. There were many different seating areas in stadiums that held baseball games around America. These varied in price, depending on their location, and whether or not they were covered with a roof. The cheapest seats at these venues were uncovered and offered no protection from the sun. Many of those who occupied them suffered from sun-burn. And that's where the bleachers got their name. If you sat in the bleachers at a game for a few hours, you got bleached under the hot sun.

There is another thing which puzzles me about seating and standing arrangements at sports venues all over the world – and I don't have a solution for you.

Why, if you have a ticket for the 'terrace' at a football match, will you be obliged to stand, whereas if you have a ticket for the 'stand', you will be able to sit down to watch the game? No doubt there's a very good explanation for what seems to me a complete contradiction, but I'm afraid – like John Williams' unanswered questions mentioned earlier – I don't know the answer.

The move to City West, where there was much more space, meant that the Irish Masters ceased to be a one-table event. For years, the Masters was an event for players ranked in the top 16 in the world and for players invited by the sponsors. It was not a 'ranking' event in world snooker, which meant that winning it, or reaching the final, did not affect a player's standing in the world ranking order. However, when the snooker governing body, the WPBSA, decreed that the Masters would now become a ranking event on the snooker calendar, it meant that far more players were eligible to play in the event. This, in turn, meant that the event stretched into a second week as a lot more matches had to be played.

Three extra tables were erected outside the main auditorium, with only a hoarding separating them, and matches were played simultaneously in front of a handful of spectators. For me, this was a great insight into the less glamorous side of the game, and a tough, hard graft for players who were, after all, playing for a living.

In the world of professional snooker, the place for all players to be is in the top 16 in the world. This guarantees participation in all the major events held under the auspices of the WPBSA and invitations to take part in other sponsored events. Those in the top 16 also avoided the dreaded pitfall of having to pre-qualify for any tournament where there's always the possibility of a major upset at the hands of a player 200 places below them in the rankings.

Stephen Murphy played on the professional circuit in England for a number of years and was highly regarded as a player. However, he chose to leave the game and return home to Ireland. He has been a member of the RTÉ commentary team at the Masters for a number of years. I asked Stephen if he ever regretted giving up the sport, and he said that while he missed the game, he had no regrets. Stephen told me that the only place to be on the snooker ladder was in the top 16 and that the gap from number 17 down to number 250 was a very thin one. The commitment and determination to make it to the top is enormous in snooker. Six hours of practice per day, every day, would be regarded as the norm. There is a proliferation of young players coming up through the ranks, all of them striving to follow in the footsteps of Davis, Hendry, Higgins and O'Sullivan.

Sadly, the Irish Masters is no longer a part of the sporting calendar. Through a combination of events, many of which are disputed by the various parties involved, the China Open has replaced the Masters. Snooker has become hugely popular in China and the governing body has sought to cash in on this popularity by staging a ranking event in that country. The Irish public have lost out on the opportunity to see the top players in the world playing here, and the television audience is deprived of what used to be a great week of snooker.

I made a lot of friends down through the years at the Masters. I remember with particular affection John Pullman, for many years the voice of snooker on television world-wide. 'Pully' was special. His knowledge of the game was legendary, and he had a voice which was tailor-made for television commentating. He had a sense of humour which was infectious, and he endeared himself to all those who got to know him. That sense of humour often had a mischievous twist. Every night, having finished his commentating duties, he would return to his hotel, take up position on the same bar stool he would occupy for the duration of his stay – and call for a 'large Shirley Bassey!'

2
RTÉ's Big Days in Croker

A Black & White Affair

The coverage of the All-Ireland finals now lasts for five hours as Irish people in their respective county jerseys gather in bars and hotels in a multitude of time-zones around the globe. Up to 20 cameras will be positioned around the ground to capture the action, on and off the field.

In 1968, on my Croke Park debut, there were four monochrome cameras. RTÉ was still transmitting in black and white then. Two years later, in 1970, a young lady from Derry called Dana would hurry RTÉ's decision to buy a colour outside broadcast unit when she won the Eurovision Song Contest in Amsterdam.

Match coverage back then was very basic with two cameras positioned beside the commentary box in the Hogan Stand, a third camera down at ground level in the old tunnel and the fourth up on the old scoreboard at the Canal End, where its lens would protrude through a hole in the scoreboard. There were no pre-match interviews, no post-match discussion and no instant replays of the action. The 'flash' interview with the winning manager was still in the future, as was the 'man of the match' award. The transmission did not start until shortly before match time, when Mícheál O'Hehir would welcome viewers with his customary greeting, which he brought from his days in radio.

'Bail o Dhia oraibh a cháirde Gael, agus fáilte roimh go Páirc an Chrócaigh.'

I had listened to those words many times on radio and on television, and they evoked a certain magic but at that 1968 final I heard them through the headphones I was wearing. I really felt that I was part of the action. I wasn't let near a camera, as I was only 'shadowing' a camera colleague that day. Hurling was much too fast for a newcomer, and I would have to make do with watching the seasoned pros in action. I think they brought me along because they knew that I was sports mad, and that hopefully, I might put that to good use eventually.

The basic rules for covering a game have not changed dramatically since that day, despite the huge advances in technology. The two cameras high up in the stand were the main action cameras, just as they are today. They are known as the 'wide' and 'tight' cameras. The wide camera had a shot which showed approximately half the field, and it followed the action as it unfolded. The tight camera followed individual players, such as scorers, free-takers, injured players, the referee, and it also provided close-up shots as its title implies. I remember being told in training that the person operating the tight camera might not know at the end of a game who had won the match, such was the high level of concentration. I made a mental note to avoid getting stuck on that camera in the future – if I could avoid it.

The camera up on the scoreboard saw the game from a different perspective and could provide a variety of shots of the action, on and off the field. I loved the camera in the tunnel as it was so much closer to the action at ground level. It could look across the field into the dugout at team mentors and selectors, in the days before team managers. Those dugouts were on the Cusack Stand side of the ground then and team officials and substitutes huddled together, barely covered from the elements. The tunnel camera also followed the action on the field and could show the dignitaries in the stand behind it.

Before the game, the cameraman would move out close to the sideline and shoot the arrival of the Artane Boys Band as they marched out onto the field. Some of the braver cameramen would stand out from the tunnel at the start of the game and within seconds would incur the wrath of the spectators on either side of them in the lower deck of the stand.

'Get that fuckin' camera out of there! I didn't pay good money to look at the back of your head.'

They were right of course, and a line was drawn beyond which the camera could not go during the game. This was fine until the crowd in its excitement would stand up on either side of the tunnel and totally block the view of the camera. Féidhlim Ó Broin was the chief steward in Croke Park in those early years, and he was one of the kindest and most helpful men you could meet – but I'm sure he often quietly cursed the presence of that camera in his tunnel.

The Shaky Scoreboard

Camera three in the tunnel carried out another important task during the course of a game, and that was showing the score to the viewer at home. There were no computer graphics as we know them today, and it was done manually. If we wanted to show a photograph on the air, we simply sat the picture up on what we called a 'caption stand', and the camera in the tunnel would shoot the photo. The 'caption stand' was a black wooden stand about four feet high, the top of which looked like a music stand with a narrow shelf at the top. We would place a thin piece of black felt backing on the shelf, onto which we could then stick letters and digits as required. It was a smaller version of the notice-board you might see in the lobby of a hotel, informing visitors of events taking place in different function rooms.

Before the game, the names of the competing counties were stuck onto the board, in white lettering against the black felt. As the game progressed the appropriate digits were stuck on the board, showing the score. The caption stand was placed in the centre of the tunnel. Each time a score was registered, camera three would swing around and shoot the stand, looking into the tunnel. Because of the uneven surface in the tunnel, it was not uncommon to have a coin or two stuck under one side of the caption stand in order to have the lettering straight on the screen. The shot of the score was super-imposed over a shot from one of the cameras up in the stand. I lost track of the number of times someone would walk in front of the caption stand while we were showing the match score.

The system was replaced by a state-of-the-art magnetic board at which we could throw the digits knowing they would stick. Later still a clock was added. This was not a clock in the real sense, but a large white semi-circle on a black backing. The semi-circle denoted half an hour, and there was a hand on this 'clock' which could be moved around manually to show how much time had elapsed in the half. Many a broken-hearted supporter sitting on either side of the tunnel shouted down to us to leave the clock alone when their team was running out of time and facing defeat in a final.

The greatest challenge for the tunnel camera on All-Ireland Final day came at the end of the game, and that was the presentation of the trophy. A strong nerve was required. In those early days, it was the only camera that could see the presentation area head-on and, therefore, it had to be used. Just before the final whistle, you pushed the camera out of the tunnel and faced it back up into the stand. The gardaí and the stewards formed a cordon around the camera, and then you waited for the stampede that would accompany the final whistle. The security cordon did its best, but it was no match for the thousands of ecstatic supporters of the victorious team, and it was usually breached by the time the winning captain got to the top of the steps.

'Is mór an onóir dhom an corn seo a ghlacadh' has a special resonance for me, when I think back to the days when we were swamped by a heaving mass of humanity during those presentations. At the final nowadays, there are cameras up the steps of the presentation area, and radio cameras which don't require a cable. The handing over of the cup is visible from a variety of angles. It was a challenge in those early years, but it was special and we felt we were part of it.

Tricksters & Chancers in the Tunnel

Bill Robinson, a legend in the RTÉ camera department, loved that tunnel. He played many a cruel joke on some of the people who inhabited it. He caught out the hapless Féidhlim Ó Broin, chief steward, on one famous occasion. Bill brought a large roll of film to a match one day and shortly before we were due to go on air, he opened the side panels on the tunnel camera and hung the roll of film, all twisted and torn, out of the side of the camera. The remainder of the roll of film trailed down along the tunnel floor, and Bill went into acting mode.

'Jaysus Féidhlim, we're in trouble! The film is all jammed up inside the camera, and the same thing has happened with camera one upstairs. The people at home are goin' to go mad when they find out that the match won't be on the telly.'

Féidhlim was horrified and examined the 'damaged' camera to see if the situation could be retrieved, not realising, of course, that the camera did not require film. He rushed up the steps of the Hogan Stand to bring the bad news to the Árd Comhairle, and Bill removed the film from around the camera. By the time Féidhlim returned, we were on the air and we waited for the reaction.

'Robinson you're a cowboy!'

He had a big smile on his face as he spoke, and we knew that he enjoyed the gag, even though he himself was the fall-guy. Féidhlim was a gentleman. He always carried out his duties meticulously, even though things were done in a much more haphazard fashion back then. He was so proud when he led the patron Archbishop out onto the field to meet the team captains, and I can still see him standing boldly to attention when the Artane Boys Band played the National Anthem.

I don't know if they ever realised it, but the boys from Artane had an extra 'minder' with them on big match days in Croke Park. The 'minder' in question was a priest from the west of Ireland. He shall remain nameless. He would come to the old iron gate at the back of the

Hogan Stand, where he would await the arrival of the band. The band was generally accompanied by one or two Christian brothers, and the cleric from Galway mingled in with the band and entered the stadium with them. Where he went after that I do not know, and I can only assume that he vanished up into the Hogan Stand for the day. What I do know is that he gained entry to many a game over a number of years by being a 'part-time' member of the famous band.

There was another tale of a gentleman from the hotel industry, but I'm less sure of its veracity. He had two tickets for the Hogan Stand, plus the added luxury of a car-pass which would allow him to park in the special car park behind the stand. But there was a problem. There were three people in the car going to the match, but only two tickets. The third man was duly loaded into the boot of the car, and the driver pulled up at the big iron gate, chatted with the steward and then made his way to a parking spot. There he met another steward whom he knew. He turned off the car engine and stepped out of the car to have another few words. The unfortunate third party in the boot now feared that he had been forgotten and proceeded to kick the boot door violently from the inside. The game was up.

'Ye'd better let that fella out before he smothers.'

I never heard what the final outcome was, but those 'in the know' swear that that's how this saga unfolded.

Dana Colours RTÉ

Dana won the Eurovision Song contest in Amsterdam in 1970, which meant that Ireland would host the event the following year in the Gaiety Theatre in Dublin. This event would have to be transmitted in colour, and a state-of-the-art outside broadcast colour unit was purchased to fulfil this need. From 1971 onwards, all major sporting occasions in Ireland were shown in glorious colour, and it caused quite a stir at the time.

Showband supremo Larry Cunningham was due to appear on a cabaret show which was being shot on location with the new colour cameras. Tom McGrath, the legendary producer whose brainchild was *The Late Late Show*, asked Larry if he could bring four suits with him for the recording, so that the lighting people could decide which colour would look best on camera. Larry was never short of a quick answer.

'Jaysus Tom, there aren't that many suits in the parish I'm livin' in.'

The new colour unit could accommodate more cameras and match coverage expanded considerably. Mícheál O'Hehir now appeared on the sideline, introducing the games. Mick Dunne, who had joined RTÉ from *The Irish Press*, became the first sideline reporter on match days. I recall one lady in the crowd watching O'Hehir addressing the camera on pitch-side. She told us that while he looked very well on the television, he looked much better 'in the real'.

By the time that first colour final came around, I had left the camera department and was now a floor manager. A colleague of mine in the BBC once told me that the definition of a floor manager was a 'pleasant bully', but I prefer the French title, *Chef de Plateau*. A floor manager is RTÉ's 'front of house' person who handles any problems that may arise on a production on behalf of the producer. On match days the floor manager will deal with the stadium director, event organiser, the chief steward and his fellow stewards, the Gardaí, team officials and team managers. In effect the floor manager is the liaison between RTÉ and the sporting organisation. There are two floor managers assigned to match days, one of whom operates in the tunnel, the second runs the studio which houses the match presenter and the panel of experts.

Waiting for the Winners

The expanded match coverage on All-Ireland Final days brought us into new territory. If we thought that the crush in the tunnel during the presentation was bad, nothing could have prepared us for the madness of the post-match interviews. It was decided that while the winning team were being presented with the trophy, Mick Dunne and I, together with a cameraman, a sound engineer and an electrician, would go to the victorious dressing room and await the arrival of the team. This dressing room was situated underneath the old Cusack Stand. It was small and cramped and hardly big enough to house the team and officials. One of the features of the dressing room was the huge communal bath, a far cry from the luxury of the current changing rooms. We would surround ourselves with the physio tables and prepare for the arrival of the team.

On our screen in the dressing room we could see the team members slowly make their way through the delighted fans out on the field, and eventually they would reach what should have been the relative safety of the dressing room. Unfortunately for us, family, friends and neighbours of team members felt that they too should be part of the winning dressing room. Add to this the scores of hangers-on who felt that they had a god-given right to be in that room and were determined to get there, using any means required to reach their goal.

There was a window high up on the wall of the dressing room, and I remember 'visitors', who had climbed up on the shoulders of friends outside, lowering themselves down into the throng inside. The crush would prove to be too much for some inside the dressing room and they would make good their escape, but this only made the problem worse. As the door was opened to let them out, another ten would frantically seize the opportunity to get in. Another way to gain access was to be at one of the doors when a government minister from the victorious county called in to congratulate the team on their victory. 'I'm with the Minister' was the password when this happened, and another dozen would make it inside.

Having achieved their objective and made it into the dressing room, the aim now was to let all their friends know that they were there. So they would crawl or climb their way through the mayhem to get to where Mick Dunne was trying to conduct interviews with members of the winning team. We often had to hold on to the cameraman so that he wouldn't be swept away, and I often wondered if Mick could hear the answers to his questions amidst the din. Those who were most determined to be seen at home on the television would crawl in under our physio table and would resurface directly behind the player who was being interviewed, waving frantically at the nation.

A Kerryman wished his mother a happy birthday during one of those post-match interviews and left delighted with himself. I met him shortly afterwards in McGrath's pub in Drumcondra. He insisted on buying a drink for us because he had forgotten to send his mother a birthday card before he left for the final. We had saved him.

A Cat Goes to Church

The most lasting memory from those post-match interviews concerns the great 'Fan' Larkin. Kilkenny had just won the hurling final and we found ourselves, once again, in a packed victorious dressing room. Mick Dunne was interviewing two members of the team when I noticed Fan standing only a few feet away from me, quietly getting dressed in the corner and oblivious to the congratulations going on all around him. I suggested to him that he might join Mick and the other players for a chat. Fan told me that he would love to, but that we had more than enough of his team colleagues to keep us going.

I decided to press him a little harder, but he told me that he was busy and almost apologised as he said it. By now, Fan had put on the jacket and trousers of his suit, but underneath the jacket he was still wearing his black and amber Kilkenny jersey. As he put on his shoes, I could see that he was still wearing his hurling socks. He slipped out of that room unnoticed.

Afterwards I discovered why Fan was busy that Sunday evening. He hadn't been to Mass that morning, and was rushing up to Gardiner Street church to catch the 5.30 p.m. Mass half an hour after winning his All-Ireland medal. One of the team officials explained to me that this was not the first time that this had happened.

'Aah, he has our hearts broken. He won't go in the mornin' and the bus will have to go up now by the church to collect him on our way back to the hotel.'

It was one thing to get inside a dressing room after a final, but in 1977 we went one better and were allowed to look in the door of the Dublin and Armagh dressing rooms before the game. There were strict conditions. The camera could shoot in the open door for a few moments only, and there would be no microphone allowed anywhere inside the dressing room, which was reasonable. The camera could also stay in the tunnel and see the teams as they emerged from their dressing rooms. I went with the cameraman to the Armagh dressing room and the door was pushed open. Inside, the team, subs and officials were on their knees and were being led in a short prayer by the late Cardinal Tomás O'Fiaich. We decided to back away until they were finished, as this was too private a moment to eavesdrop on.

Pat O'Neill was a member of the Dublin team that day and lived only a few doors from me at the time. On the morning of big games in which Dublin were playing, I would drop in to Pat on my way to Croke Park to wish him well, as I did on the morning of that 1977 final. That afternoon, our camera showed the Dubs leaving the dressing room and rushing down the tunnel. On his way out, O'Neill stopped in his tracks, shook hands with me and wished me good luck for the day.

Later that evening, I asked him what his message of good luck was all about. He had no recollection of the incident ever taking place. He put on his doctor's hat briefly that evening too when he called out to my house to check on my wife Ursula, who had not been feeling well at the match. He assured us that there was nothing to worry about but added that she was pregnant. Then he rejoined his teammates to celebrate Dublin's victory and his second All-Ireland medal. Joe Kernan scored two goals for Armagh in that final but finished with a runners-up medal, which he purposefully brought with him to Croke Park more than 20 years later as manager of Armagh.

Stealing the Sliothar

The following year, 1978, saw Cork win their third hurling final in a row, and the last few minutes of that game proved to be a little embarrassing for me. I was making my way over to the Cusack Stand dressing room to set ourselves up for the post-match interviews, and I sat near the sideline to watch the last of the action. The ball was cleared by one of the Cork backs, and it rolled, slowly, out over the line and finished up in my lap. My first instinct was to throw it towards the linesman, but he was quite a distance from me. Then it occurred to me that this could be a very nice souvenir from the final.

The decision was taken out of my hands when a replacement sliothar was thrown to the linesman from one of the dugouts. When play resumed, I rose from where I was with my newly-acquired trophy clutched tightly in my hand, delighted that no-one had noticed how expertly I had managed to hold on to that ball. But I was wrong! Over the roar of the crowd, I heard the loud boom of a vaguely familiar voice pierce the air.

'Give back that ball de Brún, you thievin' bastard!'

It was Jimmy Keaveney, hero of Dublin's great team of the 1970s, who was sitting with Bobby Doyle, his teammate in their glory years. The tunnel swallowed me up seconds later, and I still have that sliothar at home 30 years on. The following year, 1979, saw the start of Kerry's remarkable four-in-a-row success under the guidance of Mick O'Dwyer. They were a wonderful side, and I got to know all of them very well during that great run, a run which was brought to an abrupt end by Seamus Darby's goal in the final seconds of the 1982 final.

Losing dressing rooms on All-Ireland Final days are a place of utter desolation, but the Kerry dressing room that day was funereal as they tried to come to terms with their failure to win the coveted five-in-a-row. In the Offaly dressing room nobody cared too much about records as they celebrated their famous victory. They didn't worry too much about the man who had thousands of Kerry jerseys with the legend 'five-in-a-row' already printed on them. Rumour had it that he tried to sell them in Offaly afterwards with the legend amended to read 'five-in-a-row-nearly'.

PR Shake-up for GAA Finals

In that same year that Offaly halted Kerry's bid for a fifth successive All-Ireland title, the GAA invited Public Relations of Ireland to look at the presentation of the two All-Ireland Final days in Croke Park and make recommendations on how this could be improved. Bill O'Herlihy, Managing Director and also a member of the national executive of Féile na nGael, would lead the team. He was joined by Pat Heneghan, who directed the Carroll's Irish Open golf and was responsible for the All-Stars for many years.

They were a formidable team. Some of the suggestions they made were groundbreaking and, in some cases, ahead of their time. Implementing the more radical suggestions would have meant a break with tradition, which they recognised would be resisted, but many recommendations were taken on board and are still being practiced today.

The report recommended that on Final days the two teams would enter the field together. This was turned down. It also recommended that team officials be provided with armbands, or bibs, and that they enter the field two minutes before the team. A public address announcement would herald the team's arrival on the field and a team fanfare was to be played for each team. Another two of the recommendations were not acted on. The report suggested that the losing team be presented with runner-up medals after the game, followed by the winning team receiving their medals. This would be followed by the captain being presented with the trophy, and there the formalities would end with no speech from the winning captain. Singing from the victory podium was not to be encouraged.

The report acknowledged that the parade of the teams was a traditional part of All-Ireland Final day, but wondered if it was popular with the players. Croke Park was a dull, colourless stadium then and suggestions were made on how it might be brightened up for these days, which would be seen around the world. A full timetable was drawn up for the day, which had to be followed, but this met with resistance from team officials. Many team officials were taken aback at having to wear armbands or bibs, but it limited the number of people who had access to the field and the dressing rooms. The hangers-on were being eliminated.

A new public address system was required, and this was acted on. The timing of specific events during the day would have to be agreed with RTÉ, and these would have to be adhered to on the day. There was some resistance to RTÉ having a handheld camera on the field to cover the parade, but the report stated that this was common practice at sporting events around the world. It also accepted that RTÉ was different from other media, as it was paying to be there.

However, the RTÉ floor manager [yours truly] did not escape without censure, and I was blamed in the report for 'delaying the arrival of the Taoiseach and the President'. I don't recall the incident, but I am fairly certain what might have happened. More than likely we were in a commercial break, or showing a pre-recorded interview, or running a few seconds late. It would be up to me to stall the arrivals for 20 or 30 seconds. Not surprisingly, the report recommended that the GAA and RTÉ synchronise their watches on match days.

There was initial resistance to the report as county boards felt that they were being dictated to by Croke Park, when, in fact, what Croke Park was trying to do was bring order to match-day proceedings. However, county boards felt at the time that they were not being consulted in advance of big games regarding what time they were to enter the field and the number of people who could accompany the team onto the field. In the end, many of the recommendations in the report were implemented and are still in place today.

Guthrie Gets the Job Done

The GAA were fortunate to have the right man at the time to implement the new regulations, and that was Pat Guthrie. Many a steward, team official, photographer and this RTÉ floor manager felt the wrath of Guthrie in the 20-plus years that he presided over events in Croke Park. He ran his operation with absolute precision. He was not just the event co-ordinator, he was a dictator, but he got the job done and always on time.

Very shortly after his arrival in Croke Park, we shared a table at the Monday reception for the All-Ireland teams in the Burlington Hotel. This lunch has been discontinued for a number of years now. Players preferred to get home to their own counties, and it was particularly difficult for losing teams to attend that lunch on the day after the final. During the lunch Pat berated me for some incident that had happened the day before, which, in fact, had nothing to do with me. I took exception to this and walked out of the lunch. He caught up with me in the lobby of the hotel, and we adjourned to O'Briens of Leeson Street, just up the road. There we solved the problems of the GAA and RTÉ, and indeed, the wider world.

PPG [as he always signed his name] and I became friends and have remained so ever since, despite the fact that we continued to have many a good battle on match days. The difference now was that we both knew where the other was coming from. Pat Guthrie planned a schedule for big match days with attention given to every detail, and he implemented those plans with military precision. He was abrupt, charming, rude, funny and irreverent – all at the same time. He struck fear into many a steward and team official inside and outside Croke Park. That schedule took into account every possibility that might arise during the day. Key stewards were assigned to both teams and to dressing rooms. Arrivals of dignatories and VIPs were worked out in detail, as were the arrangements for the Taoiseach and the President. Guthrie built a team around him to run his operation: ball boys behind the goals, water boys on the sidelines and a team of 'red carpet' workers who were drilled like an army. He sometimes rewarded members of this team with a match ticket, and I remember him being very annoyed that one of the team did not fully appreciate this gesture.

'The art of conversation in Ireland is dead. I gave that little hoor a ticket for the hurling final and do you know what he said to me! Coo-ell! Christ Almighty, that's all he could say. Coo-ell!'

Nothing escaped him on match days, and he always wrote a post-match report in which he would highlight things that were not quite up to scratch. The following are a few gems from his report on the 1983 hurling final, and one wonders how he could be in so many places at any given time.

'Teams: The Galway minor team, contrary to all the traditions and instructions of the GAA, made a lap of honour of the pitch, which is regrettable.'

'Both the Kilkenny and Cork teams arrived at Croke Park very late. In both cases many more people than was necessary were admitted to their dressing rooms.'

'Steward: This man, not alone allowed people but actively encouraged people on to the pitch after the end of the minor match.'

'RTÉ: Even though RTÉ were present when the timetable for the day was decided upon, in the hours before the match they decided to ask for specific changes.'

To be fair to Pat, he spread his wrath equally and even the GAA was not spared. In the same report, he made a reference to the Reception Room for dignitaries after the game, and the manner in which chairs were stored there.

'It gave the appearance of the type of hall one would see after it was cleared for a Céilí in the west of Ireland and did not have any professional appearance about it.'

That was one of Guthrie's strengths – his attention to detail – and he made a huge contribution to the smooth running of events during his time in Croke Park. Being from Clare, he was certainly qualified to know how a room set up for a Céilí should look.

Jerry Grogan, a proud Kerryman, took on the role of event coordinator when Pat Guthrie left Croke Park. A schoolteacher, Jerry has been greatly involved with Cumann Na mBunscol for many years and given great service to the GAA. He gets on with match-day business calmly and quietly – he gets the job done. The only time he gets animated in Croke Park is when Kerry are playing. I have thoroughly enjoyed working with him.

Michael Lyster in the Crow's Nest

Two weeks after that hurling final, Galway and Dublin met in a tempestuous football final, where four players were sent to the line. It was an ugly day overall for the GAA. A huge crush of fans managed to get to the side of the field well before the end of the game. It was clear that Croke Park was in need of a major overhaul, and no one saw this more clearly than Liam Mulvihill, the GAA's Director General. In fact, Liam realised that Croke Park was not just in need of an overhaul. What the GAA needed was a new Croke Park. Thus the seeds were sown for what is now one of the finest stadiums in the world. There were sceptics aplenty, many within the GAA itself, who firmly believed that Mulvihill's vision would come to nothing. Even when the first model of the massive new stadium was put on display in Croke Park, the doubts still persisted.

In 1984 the GAA celebrated its centenary year, and the hurling final was played in Thurles that year, the town where the organisation was founded. Thousands flocked to the town that weekend, not just to attend the match, but also in the desire to be part of the occasion. Liam Ó Murchú, the popular presenter of *Trom agus Eadtrom* at the time, hosted a special centenary *Up for the Match* from the Premier Ballroom, where the numbers of people in the audience was surely double the amount of tickets issued. The game itself was an anticlimax, Cork winning in a canter.

The Sunday Game, which was broadcast live from that same ballroom, broke new ground that night. The entire Cork team led by the great John Fenton appeared on the programme and it set the precedent for visiting the winning team's banquets in the years which followed. Another milestone was reached at the All-Ireland semi-final the following year between Galway and Cork. It was the first time that the match coverage included a pre-match and post-match discussion, and also an analysis at half-time. Michael Lyster and Joe Connolly, the Galway captain who made a memorable speech after his team won the 1980 final, sat in the front row of the old Hogan Stand near the canal end, and Michael presented the programme from there.

The reader may wonder how we were allowed to take such prime seats at a game of this importance. The answer is simple. There were only 8,000 people at that game. The weather conditions on the day would not have encouraged many to leave their homes to go to a game. In recent times we hear a lot spoken about global warming and climate change, but the amount of water which fell on Croke Park that day was phenomenal. But it wasn't just the rain. Match crowds were much smaller 20 years ago than they are now. Sporting organisations were concerned then that too many games on television would keep crowd numbers down. As a consequence, RTÉ was only allowed to show the semi-finals and finals live. The opposite is actually the case – the more exposure a game receives, the greater the number of people who will turn up to watch it.

Twenty years ago, bringing an Ulster final to Croke Park and attracting a crowd of over 60,000 would have been unthinkable. The 'wall to wall' coverage now offered by *The Sunday Game* from early May to the end of September on Saturdays and Sundays has bolstered attendances at games all around the country, rather than having an adverse effect. The quality of the coverage provided by RTÉ was fast improving towards the end of the 1980s, as viewers expected the same standards as that provided by our neighbours, the BBC, the best broadcasting organisation in the world.

On the day of the 1987 hurling final, we moved to our new studio, perched high up in the roof of the old Nally stand, where Michael Lyster presented the programme and chatted to a panel of experts. Getting up to that studio was not for the faint-hearted, as it involved climbing a very high and perilously shaky ladder. Having safely reached the top of the ladder, the climber would then be required to swing a leg over a scaffolding bar at the top, or, if short-legged, duck underneath the bar before reaching the safety of the 'crow's nest' as it was called. For anyone suffering from any form of vertigo, this was strictly a no-go area. The occupants of the crow's nest also needed to give themselves enough time to make their way up there. Cutting it fine was not recommended as Michael Lyster found out with near disastrous consequences.

Michael got caught up in match-day traffic on his way to a semi-final one Sunday and arrived in Croke Park with minutes to spare before going on the air. He charged around the back of the Nally stand, raced up the steps to the ladder and scaled it like a trained fire-fighter. Within seconds of sitting down, he was welcoming the nation to the live coverage of that day's games, clearly out of breath and a bit dishevelled to say the least.

After the transmission ended, he vowed that he would never again place himself under such pressure and would allow himself considerably more time the following Sunday. This he did, and as he drove along Sandymount Road he was quite happy that he would reach Croke Park with plenty of time to spare. But he hadn't reckoned on the East Link Bridge. To his horror he found that the bridge was up to allow a number of tallships make their way up the River Liffey. For the second Sunday in a row, a distraught Lyster reached the top of the ladder as *The Sunday Game* music was playing on television sets all around the country. He made it to the chair with even less time to spare than he had the previous week.

Some New Viewing Points

The studio in the Nally Stand was not the only new innovation brought to the match coverage in the late 1980s and early 1990s. Additional cameras behind the two goals provided close-up pictures of the action. They could also be used in slow-motion replays – by then a regular feature of the coverage. Transmission time was extended on final days in order to have more time to build up the excitement in the run-up to the big game. A reporter and cameraman were dispatched to the two team hotels where they recorded the mood in the opposing camps and, eventually, the team boarding the bus for the journey to Croke Park. These tapes were then taken by motorbike courier to the outside broadcast unit at the back of the Hogan Stand and shown to the nation within minutes of the team's arrival.

A camera followed the teams as they made their way to their respective dressing rooms. The old dressing rooms underneath the Cusack Stand were, by then, a thing of the past. The new ones were situated under the corner of the Hogan Stand, where it met the Canal End. They were a vast improvement for players as they provided far more room for teams, were brightly lit and had excellent shower facilities. The Minor teams' dressing rooms were housed in this corner of the ground also. However, the teams still had to run the gauntlet of the fans as they made their way to the changing rooms.

Another new arrival on the scene, from a television point of view, was the 'pencil camera'. It was introduced by Michael O'Carroll, the legendary sports producer. A Tipperary man who loved hurling, he was always looking for ways to improve the coverage of games. The pencil camera was positioned behind the goalkeeper in the corner of the stanchion which supports the nets. It had a wide-angled lens, and it provided a wonderful view of the action in front of the goal, as seen from a goalkeeper's perspective. The secret of the success of the pencil camera was the number of times it was used during a game, and Michael O'Carroll knew this. It might only be used twice or three times, as it captured a brilliant save by the goalkeeper, or as the ball flashed past him and into the net, sometimes rocking the camera as it arrived at some speed.

Another new addition was the camera placed on a hoist behind the Hill and then raised high above the stadium, providing a bird's eye view of Croke Park and the streets surrounding it. This camera position is without doubt the coldest, and on a windy day, the most frightening place to be on a match day. In 2007, Marty Morrissey was talked into going up in the large bucket in which the camera sits. The bucket would take Marty and the camera operator up to its maximum height, from where he would address the nation, trying to look totally relaxed as he did so. The camera looked down on the spectators far below as they made their way to the stadium, and swung around to eventually finish up filming a wind-swept Marty. Try as he might, the look of abject terror on his face was unmistakable, but no one doubted his courage.

A Long Day at the Finals

By 1990, All-Ireland final days had changed dramatically for those of us who had worked on them for many years. We were already in Croke Park by 9 a.m., and anyone who had missed breakfast did not have too long to wait for food, as lunch was scheduled for 11 a.m. in a little room under the Cusack Stand. That was the last opportunity for food until at least 7 p.m. Transmission started at 12.45 p.m. and would continue until almost 5.30 p.m. The schedule of events drawn up by the GAA would run, as far as possible, in tandem with RTÉ's, as had been recommended years earlier.

Not surprisingly, there were clashes at times. Pat Guthrie and I crossed swords on many an occasion in the tunnel. RTÉ had to take commercial breaks at specific times, and Pat would prowl up and down that tunnel cursing those breaks. The Artane Boys' Band played a special medley at 1 p.m. sharp, which was always shown on television. This was followed by Ger Canning and his co-commentator down on the field discussing the conditions on the day.

We sometimes took a camera out on to Jones' Road to interview people who were on their way to the game. It was a bonus if a well-known player happened to come along as we were on the road. One year we got really lucky when Mick O'Dwyer happened to come our way. He readily agreed to be interviewed by Marty Morrissey, and when the interview ended Micko winked at me to let me know he was up for a bit of fun with Marty.

'Marty, are you not going to offer me a little consideration for doing this interview with you?'

Marty told him that there would be no question of a little consideration. He jokingly pulled out €10 from his pocket and told Micko that that was all he had in his possession. Micko snapped the note out of Marty's hand, told him that it would do fine and went in to the match. It was a lovely moment.

On another occasion when we were out on Jones' Road looking for a suitable victim, a man approached us and told us that he had been to every final since the mid 1940s. This was no idle boast, and to prove it he pulled from his pocket the match tickets for each of these finals.

Arrival of the VIPs

Back inside the ground, the tunnel prepared itself for the arrival of the various dignitaries, the first of which would be the Patron of the Association. Pat Guthrie flashed up and down that tunnel ensuring that everyone was in position before he announced the arrivals to the crowd. He always tried to get the minor game started a minute early, which would give him a little buffer later if there was a stoppage due to injury. It was crucial that the arrival of the Taoiseach and the musical salute happened on schedule at 1.25 p.m. There were times when I had to ask Pat to delay the Taoiseach's arrival by 20 or 30 seconds, and the response was always the same.

'I most certainly will not hold it up. I can't understand why RTÉ aren't ready, and I'm not going to keep the Taoiseach waiting in the tunnel.'

But I always knew that he would find a way to give us those few extra seconds.

The one who was least bothered by being kept waiting was the Taoiseach, and Guthrie knew this. Pat would wander up and down the tunnel a few times until he knew we were ready to go and before he asked the crowd to rise and welcome the leader of the country. It was co-operation at its best. Pat and I saw many a Taoiseach down that tunnel over the years, from the days of Jack Lynch up to Bertie Ahern and Brian Cowan. Most of the Taoisigh down through the years were very conscious of the formality of the occasion as they stood waiting to be introduced, but Bertie Ahern seemed to take it in his stride. While he was waiting to be introduced to the crowd, he chatted with the stewards in the tunnel and nearly always took a call on his mobile phone. I cannot imagine any other country in the world where the prime minister would be heard to say, 'Lads, I'm just down the corridor here. Give me a shout when you need me.'

Less than a minute later, he'd be standing to attention at the side of the pitch with Liam Mulvihill, Director General of the GAA, and his wife Máire, taking the Taoiseach's salute from the Artane Boys' Band.

With the minor game safely underway one minute early, Guthrie had time to take stock of things and think forward to the next problem that might arise. All his good work could be undone if the minor referee felt it was necessary to play two or three minutes of added time at the end of the game. This would eat into the time allotted for the next major event of the day, the presentation of the 'jubilee team'. This was a wonderful innovation on the part of the GAA, as it gave the crowd an opportunity to welcome back to Croke Park a team which had won the All-Ireland 25 years earlier. There was a downside for me personally as I became re-aquainted with players who had played in finals that I had worked on many years earlier.

'Jaysus, are you still here de Brún?' was a regular greeting, and the kindest, I received from jubilee team former-players as they waited in the tunnel to be introduced to the crowd and the television audience.

Other greetings were a lot less flattering, but it was always a pleasure to see those great players from former years and be reminded of their heroics.

The Waiting Game

There were tense moments in the tunnel occasionally, while the jubilee team took to the field. I remember occasions when the late Jim Bannon, one of the stalwarts of the tunnel, would come rushing up the corridor with the bad news.

'Cork are comin' out early, and they don't care what's happening on the field, they're comin' now!'

This always caused quite a stir in the tunnel and had a great way of concentrating the mind. Word would be sent back to the dressing room that the team were not due to enter the field for another five minutes, and Jim would return to inform us that they were coming now, like it or not. Mícheál Ó Muircheartaigh and Marty Morrissey were usually charged with introducing the jubilee team and were well used to being given frantic signals to speed up the introductions in order to avoid being engulfed in a sea of red jerseys emerging from the tunnel.

Let me stress here that it was not just Cork who threatened to come out early. There were others too, but Cork did it more often than any other team. In latter years, teams adopted a specific warm-up routine before games, and they insisted on being allowed to carry out this routine, which was understandable.

On the day of a final a few years ago, the reverse was the case. A team manager and his back-up staff checked with us in the tunnel what time they were to come out on to the field. Having been given this information, they asked would it be possible to give them a ten-minute warning and another time-check with three minutes to go. They were assured that this was no problem, and Jim Bannon duly knocked on their door to give the relevant countdown. When the moment of destiny finally arrived, Bannon knocked one last time and told them it was time to go.

'Ye can fuck off, we'll come out when we're good and ready!'

The tension of the big day had finally got to the man behind the door, and it was a rare, but wonderful moment. Most teams want to get out on to the field as soon as they can, despite what the timetable has laid down. From the time the bus has emptied its precious cargo, the players are locked in underneath the stand, where they can hear the roar of the crowd urging on the teams in the minor game. Some players like to come up the tunnel to savour the atmosphere and to check on the wind conditions in the ground. I'm no expert when it comes to deciding what studs are best suited on a given day, but my opinion on this topic has been sought by players in that tunnel for years. It gives them something to talk about in the hour before the game and eases the tension which is clearly visible on their faces. It also passes a few seconds.

Getting teams out of the changing rooms at the appointed hour on the day of a final was a challenge in itself, but getting them out for the second-half presented a whole new scenario. This is when the mindgames are being played. Some teams like to get back out as soon as they can, but others prefer to stay in as long as possible and hopefully leave the opposition waiting for them.

There was a classic example of this on the day of the 2002 football final between Kerry and Armagh. The Kerrymen were back on the field well before the 15-minute half-time had elapsed, but the Armagh door was firmly locked, with no sign of any movement from inside. Minutes went by, but there was still no sign of Joe Kernan and his team.

Joe was a member of the Armagh side which had lost to Dublin in the final of 1977, and he was now trying to motivate his players before they took to the field for the second-half. He had brought his runners-up medal with him to Croke Park that day, and he chose this moment to show his team what he thought of that medal by throwing it at the wall of the dressing room. It was an inspirational gesture on Joe's part.

The Kerry team were now waiting on the field for at least three minutes, and the referee sent his linesman down the tunnel to speed up Armagh's reappearance. Eventually, the door opened and the team walked slowly down the corridor, but they hadn't quite finished yet. Just before they turned the corner which would take them into the tunnel and out on to the pitch, Ciaran McGeeney, the team captain, gathered his teammates around him. Jim Bannon was apoplectic and muttered under his breath, 'Christ, how many shaggin' team-talks do they want?'

McGeeney was unperturbed. He had one final message for his team before they took to the field.

'Right boys. Now listen up. Everybody tells ya' that this is a contact sport. Well they're wrong. This is a fuckin' collision sport, so now let's go!'

They charged out on to the field and wrote themselves into the history books, being the first Armagh team to win an All-Ireland. Two hours later, just before I left the empty stadium, I noticed McGeeney standing alone in the middle of the field. Ciaran told me that he wanted to pause for a few moments, so that he could try to take in what he and his team had achieved that day.

'This day might never come again, and I want to savour it for a wee minute before I face into the madness of the hotel tonight, and the trip home tomorrow.'

3
Getting to USA 94

An American Dream

No one in Ireland will ever forget the World Cup finals of 1990 in Italy. The nation ground to a halt as Jack Charlton's team came through the group stage, despite all predictions to the contrary. Then there was that memorable evening in Genoa against Romania – the Packie Bonner save and Dave O'Leary's penalty. The Irish were through to the quarter-finals of the competition. On a memorable night in the Olympic Stadium in Rome, Ireland bowed out of Italia 90 to the host nation, but the appetite for more glory days like these was well and truly whetted. The nation wanted more of these heady World Cup days and nights.

There was another very good reason to go to the next World Cup. FIFA, the organisation governing world football, decided that the 1994 tournament would be staged in America where soccer was well down the pecking order in popularity. For the Irish fans this was an irrelevance. Most people in Ireland have relatives in the United States, be they long-lost cousins, aunts, uncles, in-laws or even outlaws, not to mention thousands who are living and working there without the knowledge of Uncle Sam. For the hordes of would-be travellers, this, at a stroke, removed one major obstacle, the need for accommodation.

Unlike Euro 88 and Italia 90 the main priority for USA 94 would be to get there. The 40 million Irish-Americans on the other side of the Atlantic Ocean would provide the beds. Consider also the cities which had been chosen to host the games: New York, Boston, Chicago, Washington, Dallas, Los Angeles, San Francisco, Detroit and Orlando.

For the Irish, it couldn't get any better than that.

Most of these cities would be a 'home from home' for the travelling 'green plastic hammer' brigade. The two venues on the west coast, Los Angeles and San Francisco, and Orlando on the east coast, were the perfect destinations for those who could combine a trip to the World Cup with a family holiday. To qualify for the 1994 World Cup was not just an aspiration, it became an imperative.

The Road to USA 94

For Jack Charlton's men, the long road to the United States began on 26 May 1992 in Lansdowne Road with a 2–0 win over Albania. The early part of the campaign went well with a solid victory against Latvia in September of 1992 and two precious away points garnered in Denmark and in Spain in October and November. Two other games in the group gave Ireland's hopes of qualification a massive boost. Latvia held Spain to a draw and, on the same day, Denmark could do no better against Lithuania. March 31 1993 was a crucial day for four teams in Group 3. Spain, who led the group at that point, were in Copenhagen to meet the Danes. A win for Denmark would put them right back in contention.

Northern Ireland, who were still in the running, were coming to Lansdowne Road to play the Republic. Both sides were on equal points, with the Northern team having played one game more. There was a poignant moment prior to the kick-off in Lansdowne Road when both teams lined up in the centre of the field and remembered all those who had lost their lives in the Troubles. It would be different in Belfast a few months later.

As a contest, the game was all over after 30 minutes, when the home team raced into a 3–0 lead and won in a canter. The Northern fans were not very impressed with the home crowd singing, 'there's only one team in Ireland', and we sensed then that they would remember that taunt when we visited Windsor Park later in the year.

The Danes beat Spain that night, and now the group had turned into a three-horse race, and 'three into two won't go'. Ireland dropped a valuable point at home against Denmark, but no alarm bells were ringing. The general feeling was that we were still on course to qualify.

An away win in Albania followed by victories in the Baltic states put Ireland on the verge of making it to USA 94. The Republic now topped the group on 17 points, one point ahead of Denmark and two ahead of Spain. Wednesday, 13 October 1993 would be the day of reckoning in Group 3 – the visit of Spain to Dublin 4. Victory in Lansdowne Road would seal the deal. People could then start to make travel arrangements for the following summer's trip to America. Many people were already making plans for the trip Stateside, such was the level of confidence in the outcome of the Spanish match. Victory would also mean that the final match in the group, against Northern Ireland in Belfast, would be merely a celebration of qualification – a day out.

The Spanish Teamsheet

The dressing-room tunnel in Lansdowne Road on that Wednesday afternoon was filled with tension. Neither manager had named his team. Jack Charlton and Xavier Clemente were keeping their cards close to their respective chests. It was common knowledge that John Aldridge was a major injury worry. He almost certainly would not play. And yet Aldridge, wearing his number 10 jersey, went up and down that tunnel a number of times, passing by the Spanish changing room every time. Mindgames were being played.

There is a FIFA regulation which states that team managers must announce their teams one hour before kick-off. Copies of the teamsheets are then handed out to the media people covering the match. This deadline is important for us in the television business, as we need to get the starting 11 to the graphics people as early as possible so they can get it into the computer. Clemente was in no hurry to hand over his teamsheet. I went directly to the dressing room looking for this priceless piece of paper. The Spanish manager came to the door himself.

'I geev you my team when I see Yackee Charlton team,' he told me.

I reiterated the FIFA regulation and told him I needed and wanted the teamsheet right now. He handed me a piece of paper and disappeared back into the dressing room. I was delighted with myself, but Clemente was smart. What he had given me was, in fact, the starting 11, but not their full names, only the players' nicknames!

Luckily for me, there was a Spanish journalist out at pitch-side who was frantically trying to find out who would start for his country, and he put names on all of the nicknames. That's how RTÉ got the Spanish team that day. There is a new system in place now. The FAI media liaison person gets a copy of both teamsheets, makes copies of them and distributes them in the Press Room and brings a number of copies to the RTÉ floor manager.

The celebrations of qualification in Lansdowne Road that day were severely dented as the Spaniards played some superb football. They were three goals to the good with just a few minutes remaining. Many people left the ground early. Had they stayed to the end of the game, they would have seen a fine goal scored by John Sheridan, a goal that would have a significant bearing on the plot right to the end. To make matters worse, that day Denmark won their penultimate game in the group. By doing so they put themselves back on top, ahead of Spain with Ireland now back in third place. All had changed utterly. Now the final game in Belfast had taken on a whole new meaning. To lose in Windsor Park would shatter the USA 94 dream which had seemed a certainty just a few short weeks earlier.

Billy Bingham's side would remember the Lansdowne Road game from some months earlier and would not do us any favours. It was also Bingham's last match in charge of Northern Ireland having returned to the job in 1980. This was one game he would dearly want to win. USA 94 suddenly looked a long way away. There was still hope as the Spaniards were at home to Denmark in their last game.

Wednesday, 17 November 1993 would now be the day of destiny, or despair, for our hopes of reaching a second consecutive World Cup finals.

A Cold Night in Windsor Park

Ger Canning, Stephen Alkin, Brian Moran and I boarded the Belfast train at Connolly Station the day before the Windsor showdown. It was a trip I was not looking forward to. We watched the team have a run-out in a bitterly cold Windsor Park that evening, where there was a very heavy police presence. We were based in the Dunadry Inn, a few miles from the city centre. The BBC were looking after the match coverage, and they designated a camera to RTÉ at pitch-side, where Ger would conduct the pre-match and, hopefully, some happy post-match interviews.

We called into our BBC colleagues next morning at the ground and passed away a few hours in the afternoon in a snooker hall. We were back in Windsor Park by 4 p.m. and you could clearly feel the atmosphere building. The BBC treated us to a bowl of Irish stew, which we ate sitting on the back stairs of the stand. It was good and we knew that it would be our last bit of sustenance for quite some time. It was pointed out to Jackie Fullerton and Terry Smith of the BBC that the cuisine they enjoyed on their visits to Lansdowne Road went quite a bit beyond Irish stew. They took the wind-up well and gave as good as they got.

An RUC officer informed me that the team bus was on its way to the ground. This was evident from the din of screaming sirens which we could hear in the distance. The bus made its way to the back of the dressing-room area, surrounded by a phalanx of police motorcycles and squad cars, marked and unmarked. The RUC were taking no chances. This was 'welcome to Belfast'. The tension was etched on the faces of the players as they made their way to the dressing room, with a barrage of insults and taunts ringing in their ears from the crowd behind the barricades. But the real 'welcome' awaited them when they went out on the pitch to go through their warm-up routine. They were greeted by a wall of noise from all around the ground, and if the team suspected beforehand that this was going to be a hard night, well they knew it now.

My first priority was to get hold of Jack Charlton for his pre-match interview with Ger Canning. Jack was upbeat, and if he felt the tension he didn't show it. We wished him well after the interview and arranged to meet him back at the same place after the game, for what we hoped would be a winning interview. I pointed out to Jack that we had a TV monitor beside our camera where we had live pictures from Seville, where Spain were hosts to Denmark. Jack told us he didn't 'give a bugger' what happened in Seville, that the priority was to win here. Two RUC officers joined us and told me that they would be our 'minders' for the evening on the touchline.

Windsor Park was filling up, and the noise level rose accordingly. Suddenly, a huge roar went up all around the stadium. Ger and I wondered what the commotion was all about. One of our BBC colleagues explained that San Marino, who were playing England in another group game that night, had just scored after only 30 seconds. When the announcement of the San Marino goal came over the public address system the cheers rose to a crescendo and the crowd went delirious.

'We don't give a fuck as long as the Brits don't qualify,' was the general opinion amongst those who were around us. It defied logic.

If Jack Charlton's team thought they had got a hostile reception when they came out for the warm-up, it was nothing to what greeted them when both teams emerged for the game. Harry Cavan, President of the Irish Football Association, wrote in the match programme that night, 'I take this opportunity to welcome all football fans to Windsor Park this evening and I would ask them for their exemplary sporting conduct.'

Sadly, the crowd chose to ignore Harry's plea. Also in the programme, there was a cartoon and a message with it which read, 'Please mind your language. Help make Windsor Park a swear-free zone.'

Well they need not have bothered with the cartoon in the programme. I have been going to games for many years now, and whether one likes it or not, bad language is the norm, no matter what the sport. But this was different. It was personalised abuse, screamed down onto the pitch by fans, many of whom had young children with them.

The air was blue, and not because of the bitterly cold air which enveloped the stadium. I recall looking up to our commentary box, high up on a tower behind us. This would be one tough night for George Hamilton, the RTÉ commentator, who was brought regularly to Windsor Park by his father when he was growing up, just down the road. Being the total professional that he is, I knew George would be fine and would commentate on the game as he saw it.

It was a relief when the game started. The tension in the build-up had been enormous, but now the two teams at last got down to the business in hand. Then the unthinkable happened – Northern Ireland scored. A superb goal from Jimmy Quinn meant that the dream of going to the USA had now turned into a nightmare. Suddenly, events in Seville gave us a ray of hope. Spain had taken the lead against the Danes. An equaliser for the Republic would save the day. The Belfast crowd were in full voice, and it was payback time for Lansdowne Road a few short months earlier.

'One team in Ireland, there's only one team in Ireland.'

Alan McLoughlin's Goal

Half-time and it's still advantage to our Northern neighbours, but Spain were still a goal to the good in Seville. Ger Canning was scheduled to interview Kevin Moran at half-time, but when I went to pick up Kevin from his seat, there was no sign of him. He had been the target of a lot of abuse and decided to take refuge in the safety of the press box.

Second-half is underway. One of our RUC 'minders' offers his opinion on the state of play.

'Yuz boys won't be goin' on yer holidays to America after all!'

We remind him, without too much conviction, that 'the fat lady hasn't sung just yet'. Jack brings on Alan McLoughlin, and we check our screen that the Spaniards are still leading. That side of the equation is still to the good. With 17 minutes to go, McLoughlin writes himself into Irish football folklore. It's level. I suggest to our RUC friend that he might give me his address and I'll send him a postcard next summer. He takes it well.

That remaining 17 minutes were nightmarish – one eye on the pictures from Seville and one eye on the proceedings in front of us. At last, Mr Cakar, the Turkish referee, ended the misery. It was all over. But they were still playing in Seville, and deliverance was not at hand – not just yet.

To our amazement, the Republic's substitutes and backroom staff rushed out onto the field at Windsor Park to congratulate the players. There were frenzied scenes of celebration. RTÉ had switched to pictures from Seville, and viewers at home were now praying for another referee to blow the final whistle. I don't know how it happened, but someone had passed on the word that it was all over in Spain. Jack, to his credit, made his way over to our interview position and looked at me in disbelief when I showed him the pictures on our screen. He turned his back and refused to watch. That added time in Seville felt longer than the 17 minutes we had endured earlier – but at last USA 94 became a reality. Spain and the Republic of Ireland had both qualified. We were back live in Belfast and we needed the Jack interview, now. But then Jack was Jack.

'I have to go for a piss, I'll come back to you,' he announced, and he was gone.

Luckily, Alan McLoughlin was close at hand and I managed to bundle him through a barrage of photographers and in to Ger. It was mayhem. Not surprisingly, Alan McLoughlin was elated and he chatted freely with Ger about the events of the night and the excitement of going to another World Cup final. True to his word, Jack, having answered nature's call, came back out to our interview position to talk to Ger. He surprised me, because I thought that once he reached the safety of the dressing room, he would not want to come back out to do a television interview. But this night was different, and he was going to enjoy it like everybody else.

Then it was all over. We were off the air, and that was the end of a dramatic night in East Belfast. It was an ugly night, at times a bit frightening, and not a good night for sport. On his last night as manager, I thought that Billy Bingham let himself down. The atmosphere in that stadium was supercharged that evening, and Bingham exacerbated the situation by winding up the crowd even more as he made his way to the touchline prior to kick-off. Surely he could hear, as we could, some of the chants emanating from the terraces that night. They were chilling, and had nothing whatsoever to do with sport as I know it.

It is true to say that life was different in Northern Ireland back then. Relations with our Northern neighbours were not what they are now. I would love if the two sides could meet again in Windsor Park, and I'm sure the atmosphere would be completely different. That's not to say that the fierce rivalry between the two sides would fade. Of course it would not, and it should not, but it would be rivalry without the naked tribalism which showed its ugly face that night.

We chatted with the team for a short while in the corridors around the dressing-room area after the match and then the convoy of police vehicles and motorbikes surrounded the team bus again, ready to provide an escort to Belfast airport. There, flight number EI 4395 was waiting to fly the team and officials back to Dublin where they landed 30 minutes later. Despite the lateness of the hour – it was almost 1 a.m. – a large crowd had gathered at the airport to welcome home their heroes. It was the final act of a gruelling qualifying campaign, which had ended so dramatically just a few hours earlier.

Drawing the Balls

Less than a month later, we met up with Jack Charlton again in the more friendly atmosphere of the American Embassy in Ballsbridge for the World Cup draw, which was being transmitted live on RTÉ. This draw would determine which teams Ireland would play in the group stage and where the games would be played. There was a great sense of anticipation among the large crowd of invited guests in the embassy that night, as we nervously waited to hear what fate would bestow upon us.

People hoped that we might avoid Holland this time round. One thing was certain, we would not be facing England as they had failed to qualify for the finals. George Hamilton, who was in America for the draw, took us through the various combinations as they unfolded, and Bill O'Herlihy presented the programme from the embassy.

Even though this kind of draw is conducted in front of the full glare of television cameras, many people wonder if it can be 'fixed' in some way. The organisers can take some steps to avoid the possibility of two particular teams meeting. Prior to the draw taking place, a number of balls from the draw drum can be put into a freezer, while another number of balls can be warmed up. The people who are about to pull out the balls from the drum can then be instructed not to pull two 'cold balls'

61

consecutively or to make sure they pull a 'hot ball' first, then followed by a 'cold ball'. Simple!

We will never know if they used hot or cold balls in New York that night, but they certainly did the Irish no favours. It immediately became known as the 'Group of Death'. First up, on 18 June we would meet Italy in the famous Giants Stadium, New Jersey. On the night that the Republic of Ireland drew in Belfast, the Italians beat Portugal and qualified at the head of their group. Mexico would provide the opposition for the Irish on 24 June, and this game was scheduled to take place in the searing noonday heat in Orlando, Florida – the home of Disneyworld and Mickey Mouse. The Irish would return to New Jersey for the final game in the group against a very formidable Norway. The Norwegians won their qualifying group, which included Holland and England, and only lost their final game in the group, when their place in the finals was already assured. Only four days would separate Ireland's games between Mexico and Norway. That was the 'Group of Death'.

The travel agents loved it. They could now offer a package holiday to Florida, which could also include the Mexican game. The huge Irish population in New York would set about the task of getting tickets for the two games to be played just across the river in New Jersey. They would have a battle on their hands, considering the size of the Italian community in the 'Big Apple'.

The only loser in all of this was the city of Boston, with its huge Irish diaspora. Boston had fervently hoped that Foxboro Stadium would host one or more of the Ireland games – but that was not to be. The capacity of Foxboro is 61,000 people, which would never have been enough, considering the huge demand for tickets on both sides of the Atlantic. As soon as the dates and venues became known, thousands of Irish people started to hatch their plans for what would be an onslaught on USA 94. The goal was very clear; be in the Giants Stadium in Meadowlands, New Jersey on 18 June – no matter what the cost.

4

Good Times at the Irish Open

The inaugural Irish Open Golf Championship was played at Portmarnock in 1927 and was won by a gentleman called George Duncan from the Wentworth club. The winner's cheque for that first Open was £150, and Duncan's victory has a special place in the history of the event. Going into the final round, he was 14 shots behind the leader, Jack Smith, who was his assistant at the Wentworth cub. On the final day the weather took a severe turn for the worst and in the wind and rain Smith shot a final round of 91. Duncan shot a wonderful 74 in the appalling conditions and won by one shot. A young Henry Cotton was third and got £90 for his troubles.

For the next 13 years the Irish Open was staged at various golf clubs around the country, north and south. With the outbreak of the Second World War, it was discontinued and did not resume until 1946 in Portmarnock, where Fred Daly became the first Irish winner of the event. The Open survived for another few years but was experiencing financial difficulties and was not played at all in 1951 or 1952. It made a brief recovery in 1953 at Belvoir Park, but that was the last Irish Open to be staged for the next 22 years. In 1975, the cigarette manufacturers PJ Carroll stepped in to sponsor the event. The Irish Open became the Carroll's Irish Open. The revived Open was staged at Woodbrook Golf Club from 28 to 31 August and was covered by RTÉ.

Up to then, my interest in golf was minimal but by the end of the first day I was smitten. The television coverage of that first Carroll's Irish Open was limited and far removed from what viewers today expect to see, which is wall-to-wall pictures from the first tee all the way to the final green. Outside broadcast units were more limited in the number of cameras available, and generally the back nine holes took priority. One camera covered the first tee until the leading groups had teed off, and the camera was then moved to cover the finishing holes on the course. In today's golf coverage we have become accustomed to wonderful graphics of scores for individual players and virtual reality pictures of each hole on the course.

In Woodbrook in 1975, we were still using the blackboard, similar to the one used in Croke Park, with the 'stick on' numbers. I was based on a scaffold beside the 18th green which doubled as a presentation studio. RTÉ had a team of 'spotters' out on the course, and the spotters radioed in the latest scoring information to a scoring coordinator back at the main unit. Every few minutes a red light flashed on a phone up in the scaffold and the coordinator gave me the latest updates on the leading players. We had strips with the names of every golfer on the course, and the relevant score was stuck on beside that name. The camera took a shot of the board and it was superimposed over a shot of the player, and that was that. Incidentally, the phone on the scaffold could not have a ring tone as we were right beside the finishing green – hence the flashing red light.

There was a story told during that week, which I still don't believe, that one of the spotters out on the course called in with an update on the scores of two players called Wilson and Ping. It was pointed out to the spotter that there were no players with those names on the course. The spotter insisted that he was right, pointing out that they had their names on their golf bags.

Woodbrook in 1975 was a wonderful start to the Carroll's Irish Open. The quality of the field set the tone for the years to follow. Tom Watson, who had just won the British Open in a play-off, was there. The man he beat in that play-off, Jack Newton, was there also. Tony Jacklin, former US Open champion, did a lengthy interview with Liam Nolan up on our scaffold, and his knowledge of the game was hugely impressive. Bob Shearer, Craig De Foy, JC Snead and Hugh Baiocchi were household names around the world then. The Irish contingent was pretty strong too: Christy Greene from Milltown, Eddy Polland, David Jones from Bangor, John O'Leary, who was representing Jury's Hotel, Jimmy Kinsella and the legendary Christy O'Connor Senior. But it was another O'Connor, Christy Junior, who gave the crowd something to cheer about that week. He opened up with a superb 66, and despite a great effort from the Scot, Harry Bannerman, on the Sunday afternoon, Junior held on to win by one stroke. The noise around the 18th green was deafening and I had to prise Christy away from his proud uncle to do the winner's interview. Christy Senior would not thank me if I forgot to mention that he had a hole-in-one at the 17th on that same Sunday afternoon.

The following year, 1976, the Carroll's Irish Open was moved to Portmarnock Golf Club, on the other side of Dublin bay. Portmarnock was regarded as one of the best links courses in the world and would provide a sterner challenge to a world-class field. There was some discontent at the move, as Portmarnock club did not allow female members. However, the sheer quality of the golfers on view ensured that there would be huge crowds heading to the seaside town all week. Carrolls always insisted that they would never pay 'appearance money' to any player to come and play in their Open, so it was quite a coup when they announced that Ben Crenshaw would play in that year's championship. At the time Crenshaw was the leading money winner in America. A lasting memory of that first year in Portmarnock is the image of thousands of people following the play up and down the dunes and fairways. I also learned that you don't call them crowds at golf tournaments – you call them 'galleries'.

Ben Crenshaw did not disappoint the large hordes who turned out to see him play. Throughout the week he played superb golf, and at the close of play on Sunday afternoon he was the new Irish Open champion, two shots clear ahead of his fellow-American Billie Casper and four shots ahead of a young Spaniard called Seve Ballesteros. Crenshaw was a true gentleman who came willingly to do his TV interviews, and after the presentation of the trophy he delighted the crowd (and the sponsors) when he told them that he would return the following year to defend the title.

Not alone did he return to Portmarnock in 1977, but Crenshaw also brought with him the tall and lanky Hubert Green, who a few months earlier had become the US Open champion. This was another huge boost to the event, and the roads leading to Portmarnock were grid-locked for the four days of the championship. It was a nightmare getting to and from the course. Bear in mind there was no East Link bridge and no Port Tunnel, which meant that anyone coming from the southside, as I was, had to go into the city and then back out again.

The development and growing popularity of the tournament meant that television coverage expanded. There was a live transmission in the morning, usually from 11.00 a.m. to 1.30 p.m. and an afternoon session from 3 p.m. to 6 p.m. A second outside broadcast unit was added to provide wider coverage, and this unit was situated further out on the course. It fed live and recorded images to the main unit parked near the 18th green. It was a massive operation — I never ceased to be amazed by Mick Troy and his rigging crew as they laid miles of cables in the week prior to the event. Cables could not be slung across fairways, so they had to run up the side of fairways or go underground.

With the second unit in place it meant that more holes could be covered by cameras on the course. But one year in Portmarnock that second unit came in for a lot of stick. They called in to Michael O'Carroll, the director in the main unit, with the news that there had been a hole-in-one out on the course. Not surprisingly, Michael was anxious to get this on the air as quickly as possible and he asked them to line up the tape straight away. The second unit told him that they were just letting him know about the hole-in-one, but that sadly they were not recording at the time. I do not intend to put his response into print here.

Hubert Green brought his US Open form with him to Portmarnock. On Sunday afternoon he was locked in a battle with five other players, one of whom was Jimmy Kinsella from Skerries. The other four in contention were Crensaw, Greg Norman, Peter Dawson and Seve Ballesteros. Any one of the five could have won it but Green held his nerve to hole a birdie putt on the final hole to win by one shot and become the Irish Open Champion. Crenshaw finished second.

Hubert Green returned to Portmarnock the following year, 1978, to defend his title and, once again, his wife accompanied him to Ireland. She was heavily pregnant at the time and the baby was due within weeks. On the Saturday afternoon she was standing near the 18th green watching her husband finish his round when she noticed a lady with a small baby in a buggy beside her. She asked the lady in question if she could pick up the baby as she thought he was beautiful. Timing it perfectly, the baby started to gurgle loudly as Green lined up his putt. He backed off and looked over to where the noise was coming from, and then realised that it was his wife who had the culprit with her. He gave her a wave and a smile and made the putt. That baby was my three-month-old son, Dara.

Ken Brown won the Open that year, edging out John O'Leary on the final green, much to the disappointment of the home crowd. Brown was very tall and thin and his fellow professionals dubbed him 'the walking one-iron'. A new name on the European circuit caught the eye during the Open of 1978. Very little was known about him and I remember checking out the correct pronunciation of his name for the commentary team. He was a young German called Bernhard Langer. At the end of his round on the first day it was decided that, provided he could speak some English, we would interview him. I picked him up in the buggy at the scorer's caravan, and it was quite evident on the way over to the interview that his English was indeed limited, but that he had enough to get by. When the interview concluded, I brought him back to the clubhouse and on the way he asked me how he could get to a B&B where he was staying near Clontarf. I told him that if he went to the control office that they would sort him out there, as they had a courtesy car service available for those playing in the tournament. He did not seem to be aware of this and was a raw rookie in the real sense. He wanted to go to the practice ground for a while, so I told him that I would be going his way in about half an hour and that he was more than welcome to a lift.

He arrived back at the studio a short while later to take me up on the offer. He had no difficulty walking through the crowds of spectators as nobody knew who he was. Langer was a quiet, unassuming young man, starting out on what would become a glittering career, and he has remained that way ever since. I was glad to help him out and he never forgot it. He had a very good week in Portmarnock and he told me a few years later that the money he earned (£1,125) kept him going on the tour for the following year.

The Carroll's Irish Open was soon growing into the second-biggest tournament in Europe after the British Open and it was no surprise when one looked at the people behind the event. Pat Heneghan was the event director and there was no problem that arose which he could not solve. If something needed fixing, it got fixed. Pat had a formidable team around him, people like Paddy Rossi and later David Linnane. Von O'Toole ran the control office and never seemed to leave it during the course of the tournament. And then there was Henry Molloy. I never knew what Henry's official title was but he seemed to be in charge of everything. You could meet Henry in the morning on his way to the media centre to sort out some difficulty. An hour later, armed with a hammer and a few nails, he would be on his way to the Tented Village to sort out some hoardings that had come loose. He was an amazing man, with boundless energy.

RTÉ producer Michael O'Carroll introduced a new innovation to the television coverage, which enhanced it greatly. This was the mobile radio camera out on the course. Now we were able to get right into the thick of the action, virtually looking over the shoulder of a player as he contemplated what shot to play. The on-course crew was almost an independent republic. There were two buggies. The first one was the camera buggy with a camera operator and a sound technician on board. I drove the second buggy with Roddy Carr, the reporter on the course. Roddy had been in the ranks of the professional golf world himself and was the ideal man for the job. He knew the players, and they knew him, but more importantly, I think, he knew the caddies. We could go to any part of the course at a moment's notice, and we got to know every shortcut on the course and off it. We got to know every steward and marshal on the course, the location of every toilet (very important) and we learned very quickly not to cross a fairway when there were players about to tee off. We tended principally to follow the main contenders in the tournament but could very quickly go to another group of players within minutes if one of them was making a move up the leader board. There was an aerial on the camera buggy to transmit the signal back to the outside broadcast unit but if we were far out on the course or in a hollow we might encounter communications problems. So we brought cards with us and a felt marker, and we wrote our location on the card and showed the player we were with. Fifth fairway, show the player, thumbs up to camera, ready to go.

The camera buggy created a first for golf coverage on television in 1981. On the Sunday afternoon we were following the leading group of players who were in contention, among them Des Smyth, Nick Faldo, Greg Norman and David Jones. They were playing catchup really as Sam Torrance was playing wonderful golf and had a comfortable lead. He had a few shaky moments earlier in his round but had steadied the ship with just a few holes to go. He ambled over to us and enquired if, by any chance, we had some refreshments on board the buggy. We pointed him to the refreshments on the back of the buggy and told him that he was more than welcome to help himself. It was downed in one huge gulp, it took no more than five seconds, and he was gone up the fairway. A few minutes later as we stood beside the 17th tee, Sam had another quick word with us.

'Thanks for the drink boys, I was parched. Meet me in the clubhouse later and I'll buy you a pint!'

But we had a better idea and suggested to him that if he hit his tee-shot on the 18th straight down the middle of the fairway, that he might have a chat with Roddy, on air, as he walked down to play his second shot. And that is exactly what happened. If ever we wished a tee-shot well, it was Sam's one on his final hole and he did not let us down. True to his word, he chatted to Roddy on the way down the fairway and on his way to winning the Irish Open. That victory was a double one for Torrance because it assured him of a place on the Ryder Cup team that year.

Not everyone was happy though. Bill O'Herlihy was waiting at the back of the green and was due to interview Torrance as soon as he signed his card. This was the traditional interview on the closing green which would be broadcast live and heard on the public address. It was perfectly understandable why Bill was none too pleased, having heard Roddy, minutes earlier, ask the questions that he would now have to ask again. But Bill is the consummate professional, and the second Sam interview was fine. Two days later, I got a phone call from a BBC colleague in London who wanted to know how we got that interview walking down the final fairway. He's still waiting to find out.

I mentioned earlier the importance of getting to know the caddies. Roddy Carr knew a lot of them from his playing days, and I got to know quite a few of them over the years. They are a breed apart. I heard a group of them having a discussion about the misfortune that befell Jean Van de Velde at the British Open, where he snatched defeat from the jaws of victory on the final hole. There were various opinions expressed about what the luckless Jean should or should not have done on the day he threw away the Open. The discussion came to an end when one of the caddies said that the whole episode was the caddy's fault. The caddy, he said, should have handed Van de Velde an eight iron and walked down the fairway!

On course, the caddies are a great help to television coverage. The player will discuss the shot he is about to play with his caddy as they weigh up the proper club selection. Once that selection was made, and as the player prepared to take the shot, the caddy would give us the signal. Two, three or four fingers, whatever was appropriate. Fingers always pointing downwards for just a second or two. Very discreet. Two iron, three iron, four iron. No words were ever spoken. Roddy Carr could then give this information if he was live on air, or I could relay it back to the unit, and the commentators had the information in an instant.

Just when we had got to know every blade of grass in Portmarnock, the Open moved down the road to the Royal Dublin Golf club. In the three years the tournament was played there, it produced three very dramatic finishes. Seve Ballesteros and the happy-go-lucky Brian Barnes battled it out down the final fairway, in more ways than one. The crowd was so great that the marshals allowed them up to the edge of the green so that everyone could see the action unfold. Barnes got lost in the throng, and eventually emerged, to rapturous applause, from under the ropes and on all fours. Ballesteros birdied the last to win the championship. Two years later, he was in the thick of the action again. This time in a play-off with Bernhard Langer. Langer was well off the pace going into the last round, but shot an incredible 63 to tie with

Ballesteros. As he did two years earlier, Ballesteros sank a huge putt on the 18th to win another Open, and his celebration on the green showed just how much it meant to him. The Carroll's moved house once again, this time back to Portmarnock, where it would stay for another five years. The big move came in 1991, however, when it moved out of Dublin for the first time since its revival in 1975. Killarney was to be the venue for the next two years. The town was in party mood. Christy Junior rented a house beside the course and brought the accordion along for the week.

Before the Irish Open in Killarney, I don't believe I had ever stood inside the door of a bookmaker shop. That was about to change. On the Wednesday evening of the Pro-Am, someone noticed that the on-course bookmakers were offering what seemed very generous odds on someone making a hole-in-one during the course of the week. Considering the high quality of the field, 12 to 1 seemed a good bet and it was decided that we would pay a visit to the bookies in the morning before going on air. Quite a few of the RTÉ crew visited the bookmakers next morning. I had the buggy at my disposal, so Myles Dungan, our studio presenter, and some of the on-course spotters gave me their few shillings to take to the turf accountant.

By lunchtime, the Carroll's staff in the media centre had heard about the RTÉ bet and wanted in on the action, so the buggy made another run down to the tented village and the bookie shop. Now it was a case of wait and see, and hope. We only had to wait until Saturday morning. Eduardo Romero was out early for his third round, and at the third hole he made a lot of people very happy, with the only hole-in-one of the week. I was in the media centre at lunchtime that day and saw Romero doing his press interview. At the end of the interview he came over to me with a big grin on his face and whispered into my ear, 'I theenk you maybee have some mooney for me!'

We collected our winnings that evening, and a lot of people had very fancy dinners back in Killarney that night. Nick Faldo won the Irish Open that year and we decide to have a go at the hole-in-one again next year.

On the Pro-Am day the following year, 1992, the first place I went when I arrived on the course was the bookies to check the odds on the hole-in-one. The bookies had learned their lesson from the previous year, and the odds were reduced to 2 to 1. And it got worse – you had to name the hole. That was the end of my betting career, or so I thought.

The end of the live transmission at the Irish Open does not mean the end of the day's work, and so it was the case on the first day in Killarney. We still had to record Myles Dungan's introduction to the highlights programme to be shown later that night. In all, there were four pieces to be done.

'Hello and welcome to today's highlights from Killarney.'

'We'll take a break there. Back with more highlights shortly.'

'Welcome back to Killarney. The afternoon play from Killarney coming up.'

'That's how it finished up at the end of day one of the Irish Open.'

The first three were safely in the can, but the fourth one could not be recorded because there was still a player out on the course who was doing very nicely at four under par. Most of us had never heard of this player, as he was a newcomer to the European tour, but we had to wait to see how he finished out his round. I'm glad he never knew that there was a group of people back at the RTÉ van wishing his every shot finished in a lake or in a ditch. He eventually finished high up the leader board, and we finished up for the day. Nick Faldo was the clear leader at the end of that first day.

On the way to the media centre I met Peter Townsend, one of our commentators, and asked him who this gentleman was who had kept us late for dinner. Peter told me that he was a very good golfer, and that he would do very well on the tour, as his credentials were excellent. Next morning we paid a call to the bookies to check out the odds on this unknown golfer who had played so well on the first day. 44 to 1 was the going rate. Faldo was the clear favourite obviously, and we decided to back the rookie to finish runner-up at very generous odds. The ticket read 'Westner to win, without Faldo'. Our man was Wayne Westner from South Africa, and we hoped he might give us a run for our money. We would watch his progress with interest.

The spotters, the girls in the media centre, Myles Dungan, producer Stephen Alkin – all wanted in on what was hoped would be a second inspired gamble. A number of extra trips were made to the bookies. Westner gave us an amazing start on the second day, having a hole-in-one at the third, the same hole which had reaped such a rich harvest the previous year. Everyone agreed that it was an omen. At the end of the third day, our man was still right up there with the leaders. I drove him to the studio where Myles interviewed him. We did not tell him about our little wager. On Sunday afternoon, Westner had an eagle at the 7th hole to take the outright lead on his own. It was at this point that some of our people began to get nervous, and they wondered what would happen if Westner actually won. We reassured them that all was going to plan. If he wins, we win. If he finishes second, we win. I had to show some of them the docket which was quite clear. As far as we were concerned Faldo was not present. Westner finished his round ahead of Faldo and waited at the back of the 18th green to see what Faldo could do. Faldo hung on to the very end and forced a play-off between himself and Westner. We were aware over the few days that the word was out about the 'RTÉ bet' but Myles and I were dumbfounded when Faldo walked past us after he'd finished and said, 'Sorry about the bet boys!'

We did not reply, as he was now on his way to a play-off, which he duly won. Our man was second, 'winner without Faldo'. When we got off the air, it was amazing to see grown men and women behaving like children. We were delighted with ourselves, and it was time now to collect the spoils. I took all the dockets and drove down to the bookies. The lady in the bookies told me that I would have to wait for a few minutes, and I wondered if there was a problem. She assured me that there was no problem and that she was only looking after my best interests. She had got a security man to escort me back to the media centre with the two bags of money she was about to give me. The booty was divided out and there was much celebration in Killarney that night. David Feherty, who played in the Open that week, remarked that the RTÉ crowd made more money on the event than he had. David was never short of a quip, and he has forged a great new television career for himself in America. His wit sometimes caught his fellow commentators off balance, to put it mildly. One of his better gems happened a few years ago, when a player was plugged in a greenside bunker. The unfortunate golfer hacked out, only to finish up in another bunker on the other side of the green. Worse was to follow, and he finished up back in the original bunker. The ensuing conversation between the commentators and Feherty, who was down at the green, went as follows.

'David, this is not pretty. We don't like to see this kind of thing happen to a player.'

'No we don't. He's been in more bunkers today than Eva Braun!'

There was a total silence for a few seconds and Feherty, sensing that they didn't understand the remark, revelled in it.

'And ye boys don't know what I'm talkin' about – do yez?'

The beautiful Mount Juliet course in County Kilkenny was home to the Irish Open for the next three years, 1973 to 1975. That first year in the sunny south-east was a landmark one, as it brought to an end PJ Carroll's long association with golf. Through its sponsorship, the firm had made an enormous contribution to Irish sport and it was difficult to imagine an Irish Open without so many familiar faces being there. The Cork-based brewers, Murphys, took over sponsorship of the event in 1994 and under the direction of Páraic Liston and Pat Maher took it over in style. Murphys inherited a wonderful event and brought it to even greater heights. The Irish Open was then, without doubt, the second-best golf tournament in Europe after the British Open.

That first year in Mount Juliet I met Tony Johnston, the long-time pro from Zimbabwe, on his way to the practice ground. He was not in a good mood and was complaining about his travel difficulties in getting to the course. His mood changed dramatically when he reached the practice ground and I will always remember his reaction.

'If this is the practice ground, I can't wait to get out on the course!'

Later in the week I met him again and he had grown to love Mount Juliet. It is a beautiful venue. In 1995, Sam Torrance bridged a gap of 14 years to claim his second Irish Open title. There was no repeat of the interview walking down the final fairway. That was a one-off.

Eighty kilometres up the road from Mount Juliet, under the shadow of the Sugar Loaf, lies the magnificent Druids Glen golf course. The Murphy's Irish Open had four wonderful years there from 1996 to 1999. When the course was being constructed, workers discovered a pre-Christian druids' altar and this is how the course got its name. Built on the old Woodstock Estate, the splendid clubhouse towers over the 18th green and 1st fairway. This was the original Woodstock House, which was built in 1760. The house was enlarged and modernised in the early 1800s by Lord Robert Tottenham, the Bishop of Ferns. As part of the course construction, the house was beautifully restored and it is one of the most spectacular clubhouses in the country. Inside the clubhouse there are many reminders of Ireland's history, and all signposts around the course are in both Irish and English. Credit for this must go to Hugo Flinn, who was one of the main spearheads behind the development.

The club opened in 1995, and it was amazing that it hosted its first Irish Open only one year later. Former Ryder Cup player Eamonn Darcy was the club's touring professional when if first opened which was strangely apt. When Darcy was younger and trying to decide whether he wanted to be a jockey or a golfer, he galloped a horse through the estate.

The first two years at Druids Glen were dominated by Colin Montgomery, who was never too television friendly at the best of times. He always gave his TV interview after completing his round, but there were times when it was wiser to give him a wide berth. In those years Montgomery did his talking on the golf course, and his final day course record 62 in 1997 was truly superb.

When it comes to doing television interviews, the players know that it is part and parcel of life on the professional golf circuit. If they are high up the leader board, they can be certain that they will be called upon. I was outside the scorer's hut one day in Druids Glen where José Maria Olazabal was signing his card. As he emerged from the hut, he looked surprised to see me. He told me why.

'You no look for me! I play crap!'

I told him that I was not looking for him for an interview, which relieved him, but then a thought occurred to me. Róisín O'Meachair worked on many an Irish Open down the years and Olazabal was her idol. Being cooped up all day in the outside broadcast unit, Róisín never got to see the golf, except on a bank of television screens. And she had never had an opportunity to meet José Maria Olazabal. I could change that now, and I knew José Maria would not let me down. I explained the scenario to him and pointed out the outside broadcast unit, which was only 70 yards away. I had the buggy at the door and I would have him up and back in a few minutes. He came out, jumped on to the buggy.

'OK. Lets a-go. You tell-a me her name.'

I led him into the van and beckoned everyone not to say a word. He stood directly behind Róisín and her monitors.

'Make sure you no-press the wrong button!'

A startled Róisín jumped up out of her chair. Only when she turned around did she fully realise who had come in to say 'hello'. She is not often stuck for words, but for a few moments she was speechless. But despite her state of shock, she managed to show José Maria the workings of her complicated vision-mixing desk. He was delightful, and it was a very special few moments. I drove him back to the clubhouse, and we had a very happy vision mixer for the remainder of the week.

On another day in Druids Glen, Lee Westwood tried to wind me up when I came looking for him after he completed his round. He told me he had no problem coming to the studio, provided we could have a pint of Murphy's for him when he got there. As it happened, Pat Maher of Murphy's brewery was only a few feet away and I had a quick word in his ear. Pat moved in double quick time, and by the time Lee had finished his interview with Myles Dungan, a waiter had arrived outside the studio with a tray full of pints. Westwood stayed with us in the studio for quite a while after that interview.

I mentioned earlier that Colin Montgomery dominated the first two years at Druids Glen. His luck would change in 1998, and it proved to be a very embarrassing moment for me. Coming up the 18th fairway on Sunday afternoon, he was locked in combat with young David Carter. I was at the back of the green, and was chatting with Montgomery's wife at the time, Eimer. Montgomery misjudged his shot and his ball plunged into the water beside the green. A huge roar went up from the crowd around the green. I was mortified and crept away as quickly as I could. Carter and Montgomery finished in a tie, and Carter went on to win the play-off.

A young Spaniard came to Druids Glen the following year, and won the last Irish Open to be played at the County Wicklow club. To celebrate his victory, Sergio Garcia shaved his head that night!

The tournament returned to County Kerry in 2000, when the world-renowned Ballybunion welcomed Europe's best golfers to its links.

For many years Ballybunion had its own weather forecasting system. The club steward for over 50 years, a Mr Tom Allen, had a mare called Nancy who pulled the mower which cut the grass on the fairways. Nancy was renowned for her weather-forecasting abilities. If she stood next to the gable wall of the clubhouse, it was a sure sign that rain was on the way. There was no need for Nancy's forecasting during the Open week in Ballybunion, as we were blessed with glorious sunshine and, more importantly, not a puff of wind. There was a sense of disappointment among the local community that the course had not showed its teeth, and there was a suggestion that the parish priest had prayed at the Sunday morning mass that the wind might get up for the final day. It was a wonderful week for the club and for club captain, the legendary Tom Watson, who first played the course in the early 1980s and fell in love with it.

It was inevitable that Murphys would bring the Open to Cork, and for the final two years of their sponsorship it was staged in Fota Island, just a few miles outside Cork city.

Everyone in the world of golf will recognise the voice of commentator Alex Hay. Alex has been a member of the RTÉ commentary team at the Irish Open for a number of years now and we have become friends. On the last morning of the Open at Fota Island, I took Alex on a drive to Cobh. As we left the hotel, I noticed that he was carrying a large bag, which I thought strange. On our return journey, he asked me to let him out at a spot on the road which he noticed earlier. An old bridge spanned a river and was overlooked by the ruins of an old castle, and it was very picturesque.

That night, back in the hotel, I discovered the contents of the bag. In all the years I had known Alex, I never realised that he was a prolific painter. He painted the scene at the bridge that morning, touched it up back at the hotel,signed it and gave it to me as a memento.

The Irish Open seemed to go into decline for a few years after that and it did not attract the highest quality fields as it had done in the past. There was doubt about future sponsorship, though Nissan did step in and take over as sponsors for the next four years. It was cursed too with bad weather, and those of us who were in Carton House in 2006 can testify to that. The greenkeepers worked miracles to keep the course playable, but we had to return to the Maynooth venue on Monday morning in order to complete the event.

The next three Opens were to be played at Adare Manor but Adare withdrew after the second year and the future of the Irish Open was in serious doubt. Thankfully, in 2009 the European Tour announced that the Irish Open would return to the County Louth Golf Club, Baltray, where it was staged in 2004, and with a new sponsor, 3 Mobile. And what an Open it turned out to be with Irish amateur Shane Lowry winning after a play-off. It was the ideal boost the event required and hopefully, it will continue to flourish with the new sponsor and return to the dizzy heights of its heydays.

With no disrespect to 3 Mobile, mobile phones can be a curse on golf courses during major tournaments. Despite warning signs all over the course, asking patrons to switch off mobiles while following play, there are a few who ignore the warnings. Mobile phone interruptions are, therefore, a constant source of annoyance to players. A colleague told me of an incident in Druids Glen which, he swears, is true.

It involved Colin Montgomery, not a man to be trifled with when he's on the golf course. Montgomery was lining up a putt and was horrified when he heard the mobile phone ringing at the side of the green. Montgomery walked across the green, fuming, and made his way towards the culprit. The man with the mobile anticipated the worst and decided to get his retaliation in first. He took the phone out of his pocket, handed it to Montgomery as he came up to him and said,

'It's for you – ya 'oul shite!'

5
World Cup USA 94: Part 1

In the weeks prior to the start of the World Cup in America, Jack Charlton and his team prepared with a series of friendly matches in Lansdowne Road and away from home. Bolivia, who would play Germany in the first game of the tournament, came to Lansdowne Road and earned a credible 1–1 draw. Tilburg in Holland was the venue for a great Irish victory against the Dutch, whom many thought could win the World Cup. Then one week before the departure date to America, the Irish beat the reigning world champions, Germany, in Hannover in front of 50,000 bewildered home supporters. This was a result which made the rest of the soccer world sit up and take note, coming as it did so close to the start of the real business of USA 94. Charlton was elated, and he surpassed himself yet again with his post-match comment.

'I'm just so pleased to beat the Germans in Germany. Nobody beats the Germans in Germany.'

Of course despite what Jack said, the Germans had been beaten at home before, but they had gone six years unbeaten until the Irish came to town. They had not lost a game in Hannover since 1954. Bertie Vogts, the German manager, summed it up in his post-match press conference.

'We had intended this to be a happy day when the players would say goodbye to our supporters before going to America. Unfortunately, it did not have the ending we had anticipated. Perhaps the players were not in the mood for happy farewells.'

The Irish, on the other hand, were in the mood for a very happy farewell. The following Sunday, 5 June 1994, they played the Czech Republic at Lansdowne Road, the day before their departure for the

USA. The Ballsbridge venue was awash with green and the crowd was determined to give the team a fitting send-off. In his message to the fans in the match programme, Jack Charlton referred back to the match against Bolivia, a few weeks earlier.

'They only had one real chance during the entire game and thankfully the groundsman put the goalposts in the right place.'

When the game against the Czech Republic ended on that June afternoon, the fans gave the team a truly rousing send-off. Next morning, they departed for Orlando, which would be the team's base until the opening game. They would have a little under two weeks to acclimatise to the heat and humidity of an American summer.

In the run-up to the start of the tournament, many people had expressed their concerns about playing games in the midday heat. Fiery discussions had taken place about water being made freely available on the touchline during the course of a game. Jack Charlton voiced his opinion on this matter in no uncertain terms. Many people wondered how teams would cope with high humidity, and it was a concern not only for the Irish. Time would tell.

Challenges for RTÉ Coverage

There were 9 cities designated to host the 52 games which were scheduled to be played at the 1994 World Cup finals. This would pose a huge logistical problem for the RTÉ commentary team, who would have to criss-cross the USA over a period of five weeks. The team was made up of Ger Canning, Jimmy Magee and George Hamilton. Each commentator would have a 'minder' with him. The minder would take care of the day-to-day problems which might arise and also deal with flight changes, car hire, difficulties with commentary positions, hotels and any unforeseen gremlins which might arise along the way.

David O'Hagan was Ger's travelling companion, and Jimmy would have Andy McKiernan as his sidekick. I was assigned to be at George Hamilton's side from the opening ceremony in Chicago, right through to the final in Los Angeles. George travelled to Orlando with the team and I was scheduled to fly out one week later on 13 June.

David O'Hagan and I travelled together to New York. We would part company there as David was going on to Washington to meet up with Ger. My destination was Chicago where the opening ceremony and the first game would take place five days later. I got off to a bad start at Dublin Airport.

'Would passenger Tadhg de Brún, travelling to New York, please come to the information desk immediately?'

My wife, Ursula, was on the phone. George had called from Florida a few days earlier and asked me to bring a book he needed when I was joining up with him. I'd left the book at home. But salvation was at hand. Ursula had called a taxi and the book was on its way to the airport. I was to wait at the taxi-rank outside the Departures building, and, hopefully, it would arrive within half an hour.

'Would passenger Tadhg de Brún, travelling to New York, please come to check-in?'

What now? I knew I had all the essentials with me – hotel vouchers, two microphones and the box to go with them, flight itineraries. I'd checked them all a dozen times the night before. An old friend greeted me at the check-in office. In another life I had been the musical director of the Aer Lingus choir for 14 years and had made a lot of friends at the airport. My wife, who was a member of the choir, also worked at check-in for a number of years.

'How're 'ya Tadhg! I heard you being paged earlier. Are you on the 105?'

The 105 is the designated flight number for the Dublin to New York flight, in fact it's EI 105. I told her that I was indeed travelling to New York, that she had guessed correctly. She asked me if I was on my own, and I mentioned that David was with me.

'Will both of you bring all of your luggage over here and I'll check you in. There's a few seats left up in First Class so I'll upgrade the two of you.'

What had started out badly had suddenly taken a turn for the better. The taximan arrived with the book and David and I flew to New York in total pampered luxury, on board Aer Lingus' newest acquisition – the brand new Airbus. It was, in fact, a good beginning.

John F Kennedy Airport bore no outward signs that a major sporting event was taking place in the United States, let alone New York City itself. Normally, at World Cup finals or the Olympic Games, the visitor is heartily welcomed at the point of entry and you get a sense of being part of a great occasion. Not in New York. JFK was as it always is – heaving with humanity. Thousands of travellers were running to boarding gates or 'getting into line' for cabs and buses outside. For me, the American cab would become part of everyday life for the next five weeks. It would prove to be very good, awful, charming, rude and, at times, bizarre.

In The Windy City

David and I parted company in JFK – he was going on to Washington and I boarded a flight for Chicago, the 'windy city'. It's called the 'windy city', not for any reason to do with its climate, but because of the large number of politicians it boasted of in the early 1900s who talked a lot of hot air. A native of the city told me that – I'm only passing it on.

O'Hare Airport in Chicago is one of the busiest airports in the world. Every 20 seconds or so a flight lands or takes off from this sprawling mass of concrete and glass. This was my first time to visit the city, with its wonderful skyline overlooking Lake Michigan. The cab deposited me at the Essex Inn Hotel on Michigan Avenue, which would be my base for the next four nights. It was functional, and that's as far as I'm prepared to go. Claudio, the porter, would do anything for you, but at a price. I presented myself and my World Cup hotel vouchers at reception and was relieved when they were accepted. The voucher system was a new innovation introduced by the World Cup Accommodation Bureau.

The voucher was a very valuable document, and I had a five-week supply with me for two people. I made sure to put them in the hotel safety deposit box everywhere we went. They were almost as important as your accreditation. Collecting my accreditation would be top of my list the next morning.

All the media hotels were situated close to the stadium in each host city, and each stadium had an official media centre, either in the stadium or adjacent to it. There was an accreditation office in each media centre. As my starting point was Chicago, this is where I would find the compulsory plastic laminate. RTÉ had provided all the necessary personal information and photographs months earlier, so all that was required was to turn up with my passport to confirm identification.

Having collected my accreditation, I decided to have a look around the stadium, the famous Soldier Field, home to the Chicago Bears. Security was strict and I was told that there was no admission that day, no exceptions. I managed to persuade security that there could be one exception. I was determined to have a look as I'd heard that the rehearsal of the opening ceremony was taking place inside. It was impressive, to say the least, with all the razzamatazz one would associate with the Super Bowl. Diana Ross belted out a song and missed a penalty. Would that missed penalty be an omen for what was to come?

Downtown Chicago was decked out as you would expect a World Cup city to be, and it looked great. It is a beautiful city, with the river winding its way past the Sears Tower, the Wrigley building, through the Chicago lock and emptying into Lake Michigan. All the talk on the local radio stations that morning was when 'it' was going to happen. The announcers kept telling the listeners that 'we're almost there folks,' and curiosity got the better of me. I had to know what this mystery was that had the city's occupants so preoccupied. It turned out that they were waiting for the temperature to reach 100 degrees Fahrenheit for the first time that year. It was going to be a 'hot' World Cup.

Back at the beloved Essex Inn, I picked up a fax from George Hamilton. 'Welcome to Chicago, see you on Thursday,' with details of his arrival from Orlando. The Essex Inn is a seven-storey building, but it is dwarfed by its next-door neighbour, the famed Chicago Hilton. The final scenes in the film *The Fugitive* were shot in its lavish ballroom and lobby. Further down the street, which is Michigan Avenue, is where Harrison Ford ducked in and out of the St Patrick's Day parade in an effort to escape Tommy Lee Jones.

The main bar in the Hilton in summertime is both indoor and outdoor, and surprise surprise, it's called Kitty O'Shea's. It had a huge bar staff then, and most of them were Irish. The city has a large Irish community outnumbered however by the Germans and the Poles.

In the days running up to the opening game between Germany and Bolivia, Kitty O'Shea's was thronged with German supporters who were arriving in large numbers to support their team. I took great pleasure in reminding them about the events in Hannover two weeks earlier. Next day, Wednesday, Michigan Avenue was treated to another big parade, this time saluting the 24 participating nations. It was colourful and the Irish were well represented, with pipe bands and dancers. How those girls danced their way down that avenue, with those long ringlets and heavy dancing costumes in temperatures of 98 degrees Fahrenheit astonished me.

The Opening Game

George Hamilton's flight from Orlando arrived on time on Thursday afternoon at O'Hare Airport. As we collected his baggage at the carousel, I realised that we would have to devise a system by which we could store part of our luggage in hotels we were returning to. Otherwise, between us, we would have 10 pieces of baggage to haul around America when we started our travels the next day. George got to meet Claudio in The Essex Inn, but, like me, he was drawn to the wonderful opulence of our towering next-door neighbour.

He updated me with all the team news from Florida and on the mass exodus which was taking place in Ireland. That evening, there was a World Cup media reception in downtown Chicago, and there we met an extraordinary man – Jim Bidwell. He was a high-powered, no nonsense, American businessman who seemed to want to take us under his wing for the evening. The reception was a boring affair, so he took us off to a splendid establishment down by the lake. There was a porter at the door of this luxurious bar. Our bold Jim whistled from his car window at the man, got out of the car and said, 'Park it!' I was dumbfounded and expressed my surprise that he could get away with that in modern-day America.

'Boys, you see that building there? Well I happen to own it.'

We craned our necks upwards and could not see the top stories in the night Chicago sky. He was brash and rude, but he was also highly entertaining and great company. At the end of the night he wished us well on our travels around his country and told us that we were embarking on no ordinary trip, but more of an odyssey.

Soldier Field is situated on South Lake Shore Drive, almost in the heart of Chicago city. It's a beautiful location, surrounded on one side by the vast Lake Michigan and on the other by Grant Park. The park is also home to the renowned Adler Planetarium and the Natural History Museum. The stadium is well known for its tall colonnades which dominate one side of the ground. It had a capacity of 66,814.

On the morning of 17 June, 66,000 souls, most of them German fans, made their way across Grant Park to Soldier Field for the opening ceremony and the first match of USA 94. The Bolivians were there in numbers too, but the Klinsmann and Voller jerseys were far more in evidence. I had checked out the commentary position the day before, but I still wanted to be there good and early. Each commentary position is fitted out with two TV screens, two pairs of earphones with microphones attached and two control boxes. RTÉ's sound department had insisted that the commentators in the USA use the older, lip-ribbon microphones as they are of a much higher quality. These needed to be rigged up and hence my early arrival. It was just as well, as the access road to the stadium had changed dramatically from the day before. The authorities had worked through the night to build a pedestrian bridge which now spanned the road beside the ground. It caused havoc and hindered, rather than helped, the movement of people.

At major world events like the World Cup, there is always an International Broadcast Centre. For USA 94, the IBC as it is known, was based in Dallas. The pictures and sound from each match were transmitted by satellite to Dallas and then sent around the world from there. RTÉ had a technical team based in Dallas for the duration of the World Cup, and they would call us about an hour before each game. I would check both sets of earphones and both microphones. Then they would pass me on to Master Control in Dublin, and they, in turn, would hand me over to the World Cup studio, where Bill O'Herlihy and the panel were housed.

On that first day in Chicago, there was little sympathy from the studio people in Dublin when I mentioned how hot it was (95 degrees Fahrenheit at the time). 'Tough luck' was the general message back from Dublin, albeit expressed in much stronger terms. While this was taking place, George was down in the bowels of the stadium in the media centre, checking out teamsheets or sifting out any other relevant news from matches which were taking place in the next few days. Special attention was given to any news from the Irish camp, who were then on the way to New Jersey for the much anticipated game against Italy, which was now only 24 hours away. George then joined me in the commentary box and gave Dublin a final voice-check. Then we were on our way. 'Go, go Chicago.'

The opening ceremony went well. There we were, proud as punch, when they carried in the Irish flag, along with the 23 other flags of the participating nations. Diana Ross missed the penalty, again, and President Bill Clinton welcomed the world to America and declared the 15th World Cup officially open. Those German supporters who were wearing the Klinsmann jerseys were rewarded when their hero scored the first goal of the tournament, which proved to be the winner.

After the game, we made the first of many a mad dash to the airport to catch our flight to Newark, New Jersey, which is about two and a half hours flying time away. We had left a good portion of our baggage in our lovely Essex Inn, as we would be back there in a few days. The bag with the microphones and cables travelled everywhere with me, and always in the aircraft cabin, such was its importance.

We also had with us a not inconsiderable number of baby Paddy and baby Jameson whiskey bottles. They too were given special treatment. Let me hasten to add, these 'babies' were not for our own consumption. They were to be used as 'door openers' or 'thank yous' along the way, whenever we felt it was required. They would prove to be a masterstroke. Incidently, because of the vast amount of miles that had to be flown, RTÉ had made a gracious concession to the three commentary teams and had scheduled us to travel First Class. It made a huge difference later when the fatigue began to catch up.

In The Giants Stadium

The Irish team hotel in Parsippany, New Jersey, was akin to Heuston Station on a Bank Holiday weekend when we checked in that evening. Not surprisingly, there were very few of the team about the place except a couple of players who made a brief foray into the lobby to say a quick hello to friends or relations. Word had it in the hotel that there would be huge support in the ground the next day and that Manhattan was alive with Irish supporters. The general consensus was that the 'Green Army' would more than hold its own the next day in the Giants Stadium.

Niall Quinn joined up with us and we settled on our plans for the next day. Niall missed that World Cup through injury but he was scheduled to join us next day as co-commentator with George. Niall had already got his accreditation in Orlando but I had his match ticket. Even though we were all fully accredited, we were still required to have a match ticket for the commentary box for every game we covered. I also showed him a message a friend of his had written down on the back of a guidebook a few days earlier in Kitty O'Shea's in Chicago. Niall's friend had recognised George and came over to say hello. I still have that guidebook thrown in with my match programmes. The message to Niall read: 'How's it going Quinner? Met Tadhg and George in Chicago. Hope Gillian and Ashling are well. I'll get in touch in New York or Orlando. Nudger.'

Jack Charlton dropped in briefly and agreed to do a quick interview with George the next day, prior to the departure of the team bus. It had been a long day since breakfast in Chicago, and the next day would be difficult. We went to our beds, anxious but hopeful.

Saturday 18 June was hot and humid and very soon we would find out if the acclimatisation in Florida would bear fruit. We were in the forecourt of the hotel as the team made their way to the bus. I remember being reassured when I saw how relaxed they all seemed to be. There was no sign of Jack yet and we desperately wanted to get a comment from him before he boarded the bus. At last he emerged from the hotel lobby and George approached him, microphone in hand.

'Jack, the big day has arrived, no injury worries?'

'Bugger off!'

George Hamilton will never conduct a shorter interview. There was no time to argue about the lost interview. We were to travel in the camera car directly behind the team bus, which was now ready to be escorted to the stadium by the police. We got ourselves into position. Our cameraman opened the sunroof and was filming the journey to the stadium when he was rudely interrupted.

'Get the hell back into your car or get off the highway. Now!'

It was a motorcycle cop who was part of the escort team, and he most certainly was not impressed.

The Brendan Byrne Arena, Meadowlands Racetrack and the Giants Stadium are collectively known as the Meadowlands Sports Complex, one of the best sporting facilities in the United States. It was once home to the famed New York Cosmos soccer team, which had famous players such as Pele and Franz Beckenbauer in its ranks. The stadium seats 76,891 spectators, and when we saw the huge crowd gathered outside, we realised that even the Giants Stadium was not going to be big enough to accommodate them all.

There was no way all of these people had tickets – and they didn't. Many of them came along in the vain hope that, somehow, a ticket might miraculously appear. And all of them were decked out in green. It was a phenomenal show of strength. The Italian fans were there too but seemed to be well outnumbered by the Irish. I would have loved to linger in the carparks for a while, where parties were already in full swing, but I needed to get to the commentary position and check in with Dallas.

Niall Quinn was co-commentator with George, and we also had a new feature in the commentary box – a 'cam-com'. This is a tiny pencil-camera, erected in the front of the box, looking in at George and Niall. It was a good commentary position and it was in the shade, which was a real blessing on that steamy New York afternoon. Closer to match time I went down to the front row to have a look around the bowl-shaped stadium. It was a wall of green, all the way around that bowl, and I couldn't help but think that this was going to be like a home game.

We encountered a sound problem about 20 minutes before kick-off. Mobile phones were not as sophisticated then as they are now, and before I left Dublin I arranged a 1850 number with Telecom Éireann, as they were then, which I could call in an emergency. There was a short flight of steps behind the commentary box and at the bottom there was a payphone. The Telecom man answered instantly, and I gave him the number I needed – Studio 2 in RTÉ.

'Will you repeat that, there's an awful lot of noise at your end. Where are you callin' from anyway?'

I knew that if I told him where I was calling from, he wouldn't believe me, and he didn't.

'Yer fuckin' jokin' me, aren't ya?' was his response. This was urgent, I explained, and told him that I needed that number now. He connected me in seconds, still disbelieving. That first call did not, however, solve the problem and I sprinted up and down those stairs at least another four times, calling Dublin each time. A policeman at the bottom of the stairs had kept the payphone free for me while I was back in the commentary box. Breathless, I thanked him for his help.

'Now I know why you're so thin, and I hope the Irish win. My mother is Irish, from Cork, do you know where that is?'

I told him that I certainly knew where Cork was and that I would talk to him after the game. I also made a mental note to give him a few baby Paddys later.

That was an amazing afternoon in the Giants Stadium, an afternoon that will be long remembered by anyone who was there, at least anyone

Irish. Niall suffered in the commentary box, particularly in the last 20 minutes. But for his injury, Niall would probably have been playing that day and that made it tougher for him, not being able to help out.

Our BBC and ITV colleagues, who were quite close to our position, came over to congratulate us on the team's wonderful victory. Ron Atkinson was euphoric. Michael Robinson, who had given loyal service to Ireland in leaner times, was celebrating in the Spanish commentary box, where he was working. The policeman by the payphone was happy, and happier still when we gave him three baby Paddys for his help earlier. He told us he looked forward to meeting us again when we would return for the Norway match, and that he would be glad to give us any help. That would prove to be prophetic.

Onward to Orlando

Back downstairs the atmosphere was delirious as thousands of sweat-stained Irish men, women and children poured out of the oven that was Giants Stadium. Ireland achieved the dream, beating Italy 1-0 courtesy of a goal scored by Ray Houghton. On the team bus, the players were exhausted but happy with their day's work. Houghton was bubbling with joy, and Paul McGrath, having played the game of his life, was the calmest one of all.

The police were facing a major difficulty now. How to get the team bus past thousands of celebrating Irish fans and out to Newark Airport? From Newark, they would fly back to Orlando that evening. Once again, we put the camera car in behind the bus and the convoy slowly pulled away from a venue that would never be forgotten by Irish fans. En route to the airport, the police got word that a vast crowd of supporters was already gathered there to greet their heroes. It would be next to impossible to get the team through Departures, and remedial action needed to be taken.

The airport authorities decided to open up a back entrance to the airport, away from the terminal building, and take the bus to the end of an unused runway. The team and backroom staff would be unloaded there, together with the kit boxes. What they planned to do was instead of taking the passengers to the plane, they would bring the plane to the passengers. And that is exactly what they did. The aircraft was towed across from the other side of the airport, and it took on its precious cargo. The police urged George and I to get on the plane, but we explained that we were not going to Orlando and that we needed to get our camera car back to the rental company.

'So how the hell are you goin' to find your way outa' this maze and get back on the Freeway?'

We gave the police a very broad hint along the lines that we were hoping that they might help us get back to the Freeway, and they did not abandon us. The instruction was simple: get in behind us, keep up with us, when we take off you're on your own. They lit up every light and flasher on that police car and guided us to where we needed to go, and then they took off.

Interview with Jack

Next morning, we had an early start at the airport. Norway and Mexico, the other two teams in our group, opened their campaigns in Washington that afternoon. The night before, we heard that Charlton was also going to the game. There was a possibility that he might be on the same flight as us. At check-in we suggested to the staff member that if a Mr Jack Charlton should show up, she could seat him with us as we were travelling together. Our guess proved to be correct and Jack duly turned up. He must have thought it an amazing coincidence that he finished up sitting next to the two of us, but it was a bit more than that.

We were very pleased with ourselves. The plan all along was to bring Jack to the commentary box at half-time, where George would ask him what he thought of the games so far. But we decided not to mention that – at least not just yet. We had a pleasant flight to Washington, and there was no reference to the 'bugger off' interview of the previous day. In the Arrivals hall in Washington Airport, there was a gentleman holding up a sign which read 'Coach Charlton', and he led us out to his limousine. There was no certainty that we would be offered a lift, but that's what we were hoping for.

'OK you lot, get in. You don't think I'm going to let you get a taxi.'

'We lot' were very happy to jump in and to be taken up Independence Avenue, to the front door of the RFK Memorial Stadium. It had nothing on the Giants Stadium, but it did have a charm of its own and could seat 56,500. On the way into the ground we mentioned the half-time interview. Not surprisingly, Jack didn't want to know, and he was adamant. No way. Prior to leaving for the US, Jack had made an arrangement with RTÉ that he would make himself available for interview when required, and we reminded him of this. He agreed, reluctantly, to do the interview. It was arranged that I would come to pick him up a few minutes before the end of the first half. And so on we went to the match.

His match ticket gave him access to the Tribune of Honour section, which meant I would not have too far to go and, more importantly, Jack would not have far to go. At half-time he sat into my seat beside George, but turned himself away from George for the duration of the interview. This was Jack's way of saying he did not want to be there. But he never ceased to amaze me – after the match he came back up to us and told us that he was meeting an old friend of his for a meal and would we care to join them. It was a very pleasant affair in a fine Washington restaurant. Then it was back to the airport as Jack was flying down to Orlando, and we were returning to Chicago. It had been a strange day.

Monday 30 June was a free day. There were the more mundane

matters of 'life out of a suitcase' to be dealt with – the laundry. Most hotels in the US provide a laundry service and charge extravagant rates for the service. So, having checked out the Yellow Pages, we took ourselves off to the nearest laundromat and did the needful ourselves, which worked out at almost $70 cheaper than the hotel.

The bars on Michigan Avenue were now being taken over by hordes of Spanish supporters who were arriving in their thousands for the game against Germany the next day. That evening we met up with an old friend of George's, Alan Green, a radio commentator for the BBC. Alan and his colleagues were staying further up the avenue in a Best Western hotel, but said that they had already renamed the hotel. It was now known as the Worst Western. Maybe our Essex Inn wasn't so bad after all.

Next day in Soldier Field we were sitting in the commentary box prior to the game when one of the security people nearby told us that there was a gentleman who wanted to speak with the 'Irish TV people'. It was close to kick-off and we told the security man that we could not leave. The stranger persisted and said he could not leave without speaking with one of us.

Reluctantly, I went down to investigate. He had been sent by Jim Bidwell, our new-found friend from a few days earlier. He brought with him two beautiful pens bearing the logo of one of Jim's companies. That was the only real excitement in Soldier Field that day. Germany and Spain played out a 1–1 draw. Both sides were happy with that result, as the important thing for both sides was not to lose. We hoped for a better game the next day in Detroit and we got it.

The flight from Chicago to Detroit takes you northwards over Milwaukee before turning right to cross the vast expanse of Lake Michigan. It affords a wonderful view back towards Chicago, with its sprawling 20 miles of suburbs along the southern end of the lake.

Detroit is in complete contrast, having the biggest concentration of automobile manufacturers in the world. The aptly named Pontiac Silverdome opened its doors in 1978. It was the only World Cup venue with a roof. It's a wonderful stadium, and it served up a wonderful Swiss performance, as they beat the fancied Romanians 4–1.

We saw nothing of 'Motown', as we were airborne again two hours after the game ended. Bags would have to be packed in Chicago, as next day we would start out on a trip that would take us first to Orlando. From there we would make our first visit to Los Angeles and return again to New York and Washington.

Irish Party in Orlando

Orlando was in party mode on 23 June, the night before the Ireland–Mexico game. The Irish were in town in their droves, and all of them seemed to find their way to the famous Church Street. We checked in to the splendid Radisson Plaza Hotel, Downtown, before making our way to the Irish team hotel. There was a great air of expectation on the eve of this crucial match.

We met up again with our camera crew and with Michael O'Carroll, RTÉ's producer based in Orlando. Great concern was expressed concerning the heat and the provision of water for players during the course of the game. Even the fans were being urged not to drink alcohol before or during the game, as they would suffer from dehydration. Many seasoned campaigners paid scant attention to the warning, and I have to say I didn't see any casualties.

One of Orlando's most famous residents is Mickey Mouse and he made an appearance at the Citrus Bowl that day. He came in the guise of a yellow-capped, blue-blazered official on the touchline who refused to allow John Aldridge come onto the pitch, even though the paperwork had been carried out to the letter of the law. It was farcical, and Jack Charlton seemingly told the official what he thought of him in language that matched the colour of his blazer. George summed it up in his commentary.

'There is no place in the firmament of football for the man in the yellow cap.'

Aldridge did eventually get on the pitch and within minutes scored what proved to be an invaluable goal. There was disappointment at losing the game, but the Irish would still have matters in their own hands back in New York in a few days. Charlton was outraged at the Aldridge incident. Matters got worse when FIFA banned him from the touchline for the final group game.

One other abiding memory of that day was the shot of the thermometer down at pitch-side, which read 110 degrees Fahrenheit. The touchline was littered with sachets of water, which were being tossed onto the field right through the course of the game. George, Niall Quinn and I were partly shaded upstairs, and all the commentary boxes were supplied with iced water throughout the game, but we did worry about the fans that day. In terms of heat, George and I would encounter much worse later on.

Downtown LA

Next day, 25 June, we came back to the searing midday heat of the Citrus Bowl for the match between Holland and Belgium. Holland were stunned by a Philip Albert goal and the Belgians looked as if they would top the group if they could beat Saudi Arabia in Washington a few days later – a match we would attend.

Our priority now after the Citrus Bowl was to get to the airport and catch a flight to Los Angeles. We were low on ready cash when we landed in Los Angeles, so we took a cab which had clear signs on its doors saying it accepted Mastercard. When we arrived at our downtown hotel, George proffered his Mastercard for payment.

'I don't take any plastic, cash only.'

It was pointed out to him that he had two large signs on his cab which clearly stated that he accepted not alone Mastercard, but Visa too.

'I don't give a damn what the signs say. I'm only takin' cash.'

As we unloaded the baggage into the hotel lobby, the cab driver followed us in, his voice raised and his language distinctly more colourful. He wanted cash, and he wanted it now. It was the lady at the check-in desk who broke the deadlock.

'Get your filthy mouth out of my hotel and take your filthy taxi off my property or I'll call the cops.'

That had an immediate effect on this LA cab driver. He left. As we gathered up our bags, we realised, to our horror, that he was gone with a bag containing RTÉ's precious microphones and the control box. The lady told us not to panic and she made a quick phone call. Within minutes he was back, and he threw the bag across the hotel lobby. We offered to pay him again, still with Mastercard – and he gratefully accepted this time.

Los Angeles was founded by the Franciscans in 1781, and its full name is El Pueblo Nuestra la Reina de los Angeles de Porciuncula – but throughout the world it is known simply as LA. Some of its suburbs are known worldwide – places such as Hollywood, Beverly Hills and Santa Monica. Pasadena is seven miles from downtown Los Angeles, and there you will find the majestic Rose Bowl. Overlooked by the San Gabriel hills, this wonderful stadium seats 102,000 spectators and would be the setting for the final, in just under three weeks.

Sunday 26 June, was a red-letter day for the American fans in the Rose Bowl. The US team drew with the Swiss in their first group game, and beat Columbia in Pasadena, just four days later. That victory was achieved by an unfortunate own goal by defender Andrés Escobar, and it would have tragic repercussions when the team returned home. Back in Colombia a few days later, Escobar was shot dead outside a bar. His killer was angry that the own goal had lost him money in a bet he had wagered.

That Sunday in California was party time for the Americans. The team were through to the next phase, irrespective of what happened that day against the Romanians. The atmosphere was wonderful and it seemed to rub off on the officials all round the stadium. They couldn't have been more helpful, and we handed out more than a few of our stock of baby Paddys. The Romanians won the game, but it didn't dampen the party spirit. That night we treated ourselves to a superb dinner at a restaurant on Sunset Boulevard, which George remembered from the Olympic Games.

The Cop With The Key

Next morning, as we waited to board our flight back to New York, I was hailed by a man whom I hadn't seen for many years. He was a retired Air Force officer and had been based at Rhein-Main Air Base, close to Frankfurt airport. When I was musical director with the Aer Lingus choir, we had entertained in the officers' mess at the air base on several occasions. I was delighted to meet him, and he peppered me with questions.

'Before you go, tell me, have you seen Benny Neff lately?'

Benny Neff, a Corkman, was the Aer Lingus manager at Frankfurt Airport for years and was instrumental in setting up the concerts in Germany. I explained that I had not seen Benny for at least 10 years, but I thought he was now back living in his native Cork. Too soon, it was time to board our flight, and I promised him if I met Benny that I'd pass on his best wishes.

Six hours later, I was standing at the baggage carousel in JFK Airport when I spotted Benny Neff who was collecting his luggage at the adjoining carousel. Now that's a coincidence!

Tuesday 28 June, thousands of Irish fans returned to the Giants Stadium for the final group match against Norway. This was 'make or break' day for Jack's men. A draw would see them through to the second phase of the tournament and would match the heroics in Italy, four years earlier. Again, the atmosphere was electric and there was a wall of green around the ground. But we had a problem. As a result of Jack Charlton's altercation with the man in the yellow cap in Orlando, FIFA banned him from the touchline for the next game. Charlton was consigned to watch the game from the confines of a box, high up in the stadium, from where he would communicate with the bench by walkie-talkie.

Our problem was twofold. The viewers at home would expect an interview with Jack immediately after the game, irrespective of the result. How to get Stephen Alkin, who would conduct the interview, a cameraman and myself into that box seconds after the game was the first problem. The second problem was that the box to which Jack had been banished was right nextdoor to the ITV commentary position. This was not good news for us. Gary Newbon, who now presents *You're On Sky Sports*, was the ITV reporter that day, and it would be fair to say that Gary would climb over his own mother to be first with an interview. We could not countenance the idea that Charlton would appear on ITV before RTÉ viewers could hear his reactions to the day's events.

The policeman who had kept the payphone free for me a week earlier heartily welcomed me back to New Jersey and told me that he enjoyed the baby Paddys I had given him. He wished us a problem-free day and said he was glad to see that I was not racing up and down that flight of stairs, like I had been the previous week. Unfortunately, I told him, we had a problem, and I outlined our predicament. He asked me to show him the box from which Jack was going to watch the match. Having seen it, he told me that our problem was solved.

'What you need, my Irish friend, is the key to that box. So you need to find the man with key. Then before the end of the ballgame you gotta lock yourself into the box so no one gets in and no one gets out. You gotta find the man with key. And I'm the man with the key!'

God bless those baby Paddys! Our problem was solved. The policeman had a huge bunch of keys on his belt and in that bunch was the key that would lock us into that box and lock Gary Newbon out.

If there was tension in the Giants Stadium the day of the Italian game, it was multiplied by ten during the last agonising minutes of that match against Norway. Niall Quinn said in commentary that it was all getting too much for him. Stephen Alkin, our cameraman and I were safely ensconced in 'Coach Charlton's' box, and RTÉ viewers were first to hear Jack's reaction to making it through to the next round. There was a constant knocking on the door, which went unanswered until the interview was over. It was Gary Newbon. I returned the key to the policeman, together with all the baby Paddys I had in the bag, and we bade farewell to the Giants Stadium. That was our last game in the wonderful East Rutherford venue.

6
World Cup USA 94: Part 2

Collecting Air Miles

Later that evening, we discovered that our flight to Washington the next day was with Continental Airlines. All of our flights up to that point had been with American Airlines, the official airline for the World Cup, or with Delta Airlines. We were building up a sizeable amount of air miles, which were doubled because of the fact that we were flying First Class. There were no air miles to be garnered by travelling with Continental, so we switched our flight and booked ourselves onto an American Airlines flight for the next morning.

The flight was late arriving at the National Airport, and to our dismay the city traffic was at a standstill that morning. As we inched our way towards RFK Stadium, I knew that Dallas would be calling the commentary box, wondering where the hell we were. Maurice Reidy, the RTÉ team leader in Dallas, called us on our mobile, and we explained our predicament, omitting to mention that we had changed flights. There was no more than 40 minutes to spare when we arrived at the commentary box, mightily relieved. About 30 seconds after kick-off, I answered a phone call from Dallas. It was Tim O'Connor, then head of RTÉ Sport. He only spoke three words, and they were, 'Read my lips' and he hung up. Tim knew what we were up to and that was his way of letting us know!

The game itself gave us the best goal of the tournament, and one of the biggest shocks of the tournament too. The Kingdom of Saudi Arabia defeated Belgium 1–0 in a game where the Belgians had 41 shots on goal. Washington was still gridlocked after the game as we made our way back to the airport. There was concern among staff at the airport about thunderstorms in the area, but while we were waiting in the First Class boarding lounge, we met the flight captain. He was very reassuring about our prospects of getting out of Washington that evening, despite the weather warning.

'Don't you guys worry, I'll find a hole in that cloud and get us the hell outta here.'

A short while later we boarded the aircraft and pulled away from the terminal building. I was exhausted and decided to have a quick forty winks. When I awoke, I assumed the aircraft was taxiing into the terminal at Newark airport. I'd slept through the entire flight. That was too good to be true. Our flight, in fact, hadn't taken off at all and we were in the middle of a lightning storm, which had closed the airport. Not only were we facing a weather problem, we were also up against a time problem. Because of noise restriction regulations, Washington National Airport closed to all out-going flights at 10 p.m., and it was now 8.30 p.m. There was no let-up in the storm. An hour later we were back in the terminal building.

The airport had closed for the night. George and I had no game the next day, so the problem was not too acute for us, but that great sports journalist, the late Peter Ball, who was with us on the flight, was due to travel back to Orlando with the Irish team the next morning. Peter was worried. I phoned Washington train station to enquire about the train service to New York that night.

'Yes sir, there's a train at 11.30 p.m. Yes sir, there is food available on board, and could I have your credit card number?'

I made the reservations and we were back in business. As we made our way back out of the airport, George spotted the Hertz car hire office. Before there was time to argue, he was in the line of people looking for a car. This was not a good idea, but George is a very determined man. The gentleman at the Hertz counter really did not want to be on duty that night. When George eventually got to him, he was greeted with a terse five words.

'I ain't got no car.'

George gave him his Hertz Gold Card and tried again.

'That's very pretty. Now show me a Platinum card and you gotta car.'

This man should never have been allowed to deal with members of the public. We asked him why he could not put up a sign to say there were no cars available. He explained that he wasn't allowed to put up a sign, as it was against airport regulations. As we left the Hertz office, we noticed a large sign on a wall which read; 'Hertz Car-hire. Cars available 24 hours a day.'

We both agreed that this was in breach of airport regulations, so we removed it and brought it in to the Hertz man at the desk. This elicited a cheer from other would-be customers who were being treated with the same indifference as we were. Poor Peter Ball must have been wondering what he was doing in the company of such crazy fellow-travellers. And, of course, we missed the train we were meant to be on, and finished up instead on a mail train which did not leave until 2 a.m. It was almost 7 a.m. when we reached our hotel. Thankfully Peter made his flight – glad to be rid of us, no doubt!

Don't Turn Left!

There were three days of respite before our next match, which was back on the west coast, and they were welcome. In the 12 days since we started on our travels, we had taken 11 flights, and had been to the west coast and back. Two days later, I found myself back in Washington in the Days Hotel in Crystal City. Extra hotel vouchers were being sent by courier from Dallas, and had to be picked up in Washington. It afforded me the opportunity to pay a short visit to the Smithsonian Institute and also to see the famous Iwo Jima monument.

It was late at night the first time we visited the Holiday Inn in Los

Angeles where we'd had the altercation with the cab driver with the 'filthy mouth'. There wasn't much time to take in our surroundings on that visit, and we had left early next day. However, on this, our second time around, we arrived in the early evening and had more time to acquaint ourselves with the geography of the place. From our hotel rooms, we could see large white structures which looked like igloos, and we both remarked on them when we met in the lobby to head out for food. The porter in the lobby uttered a word of caution to us before we left.

'If you guys are goin' out tonight, you don't wanna turn left. Make sure you turn right.'

Not surprisingly, we asked him if he would care to explain what he meant. He was not trying to run down his place of employment, but we were World Cup visitors and he wanted us to be safe.

'Turnin' left is not where you wanna be; lotta drug stuff down there. Only go right.'

We took his advice, and later made sure we took a cab back to the hotel. The cab driver told us that the igloo-type dwellings catered for the addicts in the area, of which there were many it would appear. Back in the hotel, there were other media and television people who were none too happy with this particular location.

Sunday 3 July was a sweltering day as we boarded the media shuttle to go to the Rose Bowl. Everyone on the shuttle agreed that this should be one of the games of the tournament. Argentina, now minus Maradona, were facing the Romanians, with the talents of Hagi. Kick-off was scheduled for 1.35 p.m. but by 11.30 a.m. the temperature was already well above 100 degrees Fahrenheit and rising. In the media centre, people were advised to bring lots of water with them and to stay indoors for as long as possible.

The commentary position was like a furnace. As match time approached, the temperature rose to 114 degrees Fahrenheit. George faced another difficulty too. With the sun beating down directly on him, he was having problems seeing the screen in front of him. We solved that by draping a wet towel over his head and the screen, almost like a mini-tent. This was not very satisfactory, as his view of the field of play was hampered. Both TV screens in the box had cardboard covers around them to protect them from the heat. We removed the cardboard cover from one of the screens and put it around George's head, and it was perfect. He looked ridiculous, but it solved the problem.

Unfortunately for George, his head was now enclosed in a sauna and the temperature outside the cardboard box around his head was still rising. One of the officials in the commentary area informed me that the protective box around the screen should not have been removed. I asked him which was more important, his screen or my colleague.

At half-time, George fled for 10 minutes into the shade. When he started the stopwatch for the second-half, we noticed that the mercury in the watch had congealed in the heat and was now a large silver blob. We were told that the temperature had peaked at 118 degrees Fahrenheit, and that at pitch-level it was 124 degrees Fahrenheit. It was a freak day climatically for Los Angeles and we left the Rose Bowl drained. The magic of Hagi and his teammates prevailed in a wonderful game. Maradona was consoled by his girlfriend in the press area just behind us. It was a tragic sight.

It was time to set about the business of getting out of our downtown hotel. We both made separate calls to the World Cup accommodation office to inform them that we were checking out of the hotel, that we did not want to spend another night there.

'No sir you can't do that. Once you've been assigned to an hotel you gotta stay there sir. Sorry, but that's it.'

We pointed out that the area surrounding the hotel was totally unsafe and that there was no question of us staying on there.

'Well sir, we've had no complaints from any of the other media personnel staying there.'

Many of our colleagues staying there had expressed their concerns to us about the area, not the hotel. They simply had not bothered to do anything about it. We informed the accommodation office that we were now in the lobby, ready to leave, and asked them what other officially designated hotel we should go to. Reluctantly, they suggested we go to the Red Lion Hotel and to call again when we got there. The Red Lion Hotel on West Glenoaks Boulevard, Glendale, is a towering and very impressive building from the outside. It had opened its doors only two years earlier and had every facility one could ask for. It was just five minutes away from the Rose Bowl. By the time we got there, there were two rooms registered in our names. This would be our new base in Los Angeles. We were greatly pleased with ourselves.

The Hosts Face Brazil

4 July is Independence Day in the United States, a national holiday which they celebrate in style as only the Americans can. That 4 July, their patriotism and national fervour reached new heights in Stanford Stadium, Palo Alto, 33 kilometres south of San Francisco. Team USA were facing the might of Brazil in the high noon heat of California with a place in the quarter-finals at stake. It was a huge occasion in the life of this fledgling soccer nation. The American press devoted pages of coverage to the game in the morning papers. On our early-morning flight northwards to San Francisco, I browsed through the sports section of *The Los Angeles Times*. In her article, Julie Cart did not hold out too much hope for the Americans.

> *What scrap of optimism is there to which the U.S. World Cup team can cling, going into today's second-round match against three-times world champions Brazil? What filament of hope dangles like a lifeline before the most*

*important game in U.S. soccer history? The truth is that
beyond the on-a-given-day-axioms and underneath the
pop psychology positive-thinking burbling, lies the brutal
reality of the moment. An inexperienced U.S. team of
largely amateur players will line up against the most
talented and most creative soccer team on Earth.*

Now that's hardly the ringing endorsement a team would need to read
facing into such a vital game. There was another story in *The Los Angeles
Times* that Randy Attaway, the Mayor of Los Gatos where the Brazilian
team was based, brought in 175 law enforcement officers from
surrounding areas in anticipation of a victory. There was a considerable
amount of 'snickering from the international media'. To prove this, the
paper published part of an article by Paul Wilson of *The Observer*.

*The script is unimprovable. America, the giant nation
with the pygmy soccer team, defies all expectations to
reach the last 16 of the World Cup it is hosting. The
opponents; the great and glamorous Brazil, the one name
in soccer potent enough to penetrate even the North
American sports consciousness. The date; the fourth of
July. What other? Can America win? Of course not. Even
the Disney Studios would laugh at such a scenario.
Having lived a brief and eventful life and caught the
public imagination with their run for freedom, the soccer
outlaws will meet a sticky but visually satisfying end at the
hands of too many South Americans. Just like Butch
Cassidy and the Sundance Kid. Who are these guys,
anyway?'*

84,147 spectators packed themselves into Stanford Stadium to see the
game. For 72 minutes the Americans kept the dream alive. Reduced to
10 men, Brazil were kept at bay but were rescued by Bebeto who scored
the goal that would send them to Dallas 5 days later. We would see them

there. It was a fantastic occasion. The crowd rose to Team USA as they did a lap of honour after the game and bade farewell to the World Cup. The Brazil fans celebrated wildly and did their samba all the way out of the stadium. They too contributed in no small way to the party on Independence Day.

American TV Coverage

4 July was a big day for the Irish too, and we tried to keep a watchful eye on events in Dallas, where the Irish team faced its old adversary, Holland. At the airport in San Francisco, we heard that the Irish had lost and the World Cup odyssey was over for the Green Army. It was a huge disappointment for us, not least because had the Irish won, their next game would have been a quarter-final against the Brazilians in Dallas. That was our next game. We flew back to Los Angeles.

Large crowds gathered in the bars of Los Angeles the next day. There is a large Hispanic community in California, and Mexico were playing Bulgaria in the Giants Stadium. The Mexicans take their football seriously and we couldn't help but be drawn to the TV to watch the penalty shootout. Bulgaria won the shootout, and the Mexicans were inconsolable. Italy were now the only side remaining in the tournament from the original group that included Ireland.

The American public were captivated by another sporting event in those weeks of the World Cup, and that was the Tour de France. Greg LeMond was the first American to win the tour in 1986 after an epic duel with the legendary Bernard Hinault, already a five-time winner of the famous race. The Californian became a legend. The following year he was seriously injured in a hunting accident, but he returned in 1989 to take the famous yellow jersey – no mean achievement considering he had 37 shotgun pellets in his body.

LeMond won the tour again in 1990, and by now he was an icon.

During those World Cup weeks in Los Angeles, the Tour screamed out of every bar. But it was exasperating to watch the race, particularly the mountain stages, where so much can happen so quickly. It was more a case of watching a commercial break which was interrupted by a cycle race every now and again.

Commercials during World Cup games had been an issue in the run-up to the tournament. There was talk of the games being divided into four quarters to allow for more commercial breaks, but FIFA rejected this out of hand. However, some of the American networks found ways around the problem. For example, if a free kick was awarded close to goal in a game, a cartoon of a Coca-Cola truck would empty six bottles of Coke onto the screen. These bottles would then line up as a defensive wall for the free kick, obscuring the real wall of players on the field. Just before the free was due to be taken, the bottles would disappear, right and left, off the TV screen. It was funny the first few times you saw it, then it became an annoying distraction. One channel promised 'commercial-free coverage' of all games. They omitted to mention that the match commentaries would be in Spanish only.

Encore! The Three Tenors

Back in Los Angeles, George and I had three days to enjoy the comforts of the Red Lion Hotel and have a break from airports and games. We did the tourist trips, and behaved like two ten-year-olds at Universal Studios, the famous theme park packed with various rides and film sets. I loved it. A rumour that we had heard a few days earlier needed to be checked out too.

During Italia 90 tenors Jose Carreras, Placido Domingo and Luciano Pavarotti had performed together on stage at the Baths of Caracalla in Rome on the eve of the final. The subsequent home video and album became the highest-selling classical release of all time.

Another concert was planned for Dodger Stadium, Los Angeles the night before the final, 16 July. What we had heard was that any television network that had bought the rights to transmit the concert was entitled to tickets for the event. If that were the case, then RTÉ, who had bought the concert rights, was entitled to those tickets, and we would be more than happy to represent the station at such a concert.

A call to the concert office confirmed what we had heard. All we had to do was show proof of who we were, present our accreditation and the tickets would be delivered to our hotel. This we did, and the tickets duly arrived, not in an envelope as one might expect, but in a box. The box contained three bags which, when folded over in a particular way, became three cushions. The bags also had a number of pockets which contained opera glasses, a CD of four of the arias to be performed, and not two, but three tickets for *Encore! The Three Tenors*. They were priced at $1,000 per ticket and we would be in the VIP section of the audience. It was a good day's work.

Delta Airlines, Flight 748, took us to Dallas on the morning of 8 July for the quarter-final between Holland and Brazil. This would be the first opportunity to meet up with the rest of the RTÉ team who were based in the International Broadcast Centre for the duration of the tournament. For the previous three weeks, we had been at the end of a phone or a microphone from eight cities scattered across America. Mary Banks met us at the airport and took us to The Emerald Valley Apartments on West Valley Ranch just outside Dallas. The team in the International Broadcast Centre each had their own apartment in this complex for the duration of their stay. We availed of the excellent laundry facilities in the apartment and planned to iron some clothes later. But for now, Head of RTÉ Sport, Tim O'Connor, was taking us out for dinner. We wondered if there would be any mention of his 'read my lips' phone call to Washington.

It was a real Texas night out, complete with Stetsons, cowboy boots and huge steaks. The Dallas crew was able to tell us about the enormous audiences watching the coverage back in Ireland. They also recommended that we visit the Sixth Floor Museum in downtown Dallas the next day before we went to the stadium. The museum is situated in the famous Texas Book Depository, from where Lee Harvey Oswald shot President Kennedy in 1963.

Back at the apartment we reluctantly ironed some clothes, much later than planned. Tim dropped us off at the museum early next morning and it was everything they had said it was. The visitor stands at Oswald's window, where there is a rifle and spent cartridges lying on the floor. There are diagrams showing the route of the motorcade. There is also an excellent video presentation which allows the visitor to make up one's own mind on what did, or did not, happen on that November day in 1963. Afterwards, back down in the street we stood on the famed grassy knoll and walked up Dealey Plaza. It was like being in a time-warp, and it was wonderful. But a quarter-final awaited us in the Cotton Bowl, located in the historic Fair Park district of Dallas.

63,500 watched a smashing game in the Cotton Bowl. Brazil took a two-goal lead but the Dutch levelled with less than a quarter of an hour to go. A free kick from Branco won it for the Brazilians and sent them into yet another World Cup semi-final. I recall Barry Davies from the BBC saying later, 'if only the Dutch had more belief'.

After the game there was time for a quick visit to the International Broadcast Centre, a labyrinth of studios, offices, satellite dishes and what seemed a never-ending line of television monitors. This was the hub, and it was from here that the world received its coverage of the World Cup. Then it was on to the airport to catch a flight to San Francisco. Sweden and Romania were playing at Palo Alto the next day. We were flying with American Airlines and we noticed in the car on the way to Dallas-Fort Worth Airport that the airline had an earlier flight to San Francisco which, if there were seats available, we might just make. The gentleman at check-in did the paperwork in record time and told us to 'go like hell' and we might just get on board. Sadly, the gentleman at the gate was in no such mood. Even though the aircraft was still at the stand, we would have to wait two hours for the next flight. We were not too pleased with American Airlines, but it would get much worse before the night was over. Dinner at Dallas airport is not something that I would recommend to anyone, and we eventually boarded our flight which would land in San Francisco just before 11.30 p.m. Both of us slept for the entire journey.

Baggage Incident and the Police

The airport in San Francisco was almost deserted. As we walked away from the baggage carousel, we noticed that a bag belonging to George was covered in a thick, oily substance. This we did not need. It was midnight and kick-off next day was at 12.35 p.m. The lady at the American Airlines desk was none too helpful when we approached her with our problem.

'Come back in the morning. There's nothing I can do for you right now sir.'

We opened the bag, and to our dismay, discovered that the oil had leaked inside and had badly soiled some of George's clothes. She was unperturbed, but she did make another offer.

'I can give you $100 for the damage to your property, or you come back in the morning. Sorry, but that's it.'

We pointed out that we were First Class passengers and showed her the vast amount of miles we had flown with the airline in the previous few weeks. This had no effect on her whatsoever. In fact, it seemed to stiffen her resolve even more. She refused to give us the name and phone number of the person we might call the next day to deal with the problem.

'I'm not at liberty to give you any phone numbers of American Airlines staff.'

It was getting heated now. We noticed a gentleman in the inner office who was watching proceedings very carefully. He was now on the phone in a very animated state. He was calling the police. This had taken a turn for the worst. Two burly policemen arrived and separated George and I. The realisation dawned on us, very quickly, that these boys were going about their business in a serious manner. They grilled us individually and demanded that we give them our home addresses, home phone numbers, where we were coming from and where we were going. We told them that we had a legitimate complaint which we were entitled to pursue and that we would continue to do so.

'Right guys, now here's the deal. We got all night, and we can take you down to the precinct and straighten this out down there.'

That was not a problem for us, we told them, as we had all night too and were only trying to resolve the problem. At this point, the airline staff realised that this was going too far. We were given the name and the phone number of a person whom we could call the next day. That was all we had wanted in the first place. The two policemen frog-marched us out to the nearest cab and refused to leave until the cab pulled away. It was a very unnerving experience and both of us were quite shaken by it.

Next morning, 10 July on our way to Stanford Stadium, we decided to call the Irish Consulate in San Francisco. The events of the previous night worried us and we sought advice. The staff at the consulate could not have been more helpful and said they would investigate and call us back. They had one query though, which they needed to ask. Was there any alcohol involved the night before? Fair question, and they were relieved when we assured them that there certainly was not.

Sweden and Romania served up a terrific game which finished up level after extra time. The penalty shootout was memorable for the antics of Tomas Ravelli, the Swedish goalkeeper, but he did manage to save two of the Romanian penalties, and Hagi and his men were out. In the car park after the game the Romanians were distraught. They had been wonderful right through the tournament, but were now on their way home.

Resolving the Problem

After the game, George suggested we visit a pub restaurant in downtown San Francisco, which he said, was the 'in place' to be. U2 were regular visitors to the place, he had heard. We were the only two people in the bar when the Irish consulate called us. They had confirmed the events of the night before and gave us some uncomfortable news. Both of our names were logged in the Airport Police Precinct and would remain on record for up to three years. This was serious.

Earlier in the day, American Airlines told us that 'this kind of thing simply does not happen' but that they would investigate it. After the call from the consulate, we let the airline know what we had just been told. They began to sit up and take notice.

San Francisco is a wonderful city and we became tourists again for a few days. The hotel was excellent and was only 20 minutes travel time from downtown San Francisco. George was making his first visit to the city and was anxious to see the famed Golden Gate Bridge. He was in for a disappointment, as the San Francisco landmark was shrouded in fog. Despite its size, it could not be seen. We went to Alcatraz and Chinatown and did all the things tourists are meant to do.

American Airlines called to tell us that they were sending a car to pick up the damaged bag and the soiled clothes. Slowly, we were making progress. A few hours later the bag and the clothes were returned in pristine condition. We noticed that they had paid $128 to have the job done. This was 28 dollars more than they had offered us in the first place. They then invited us to a meeting to discuss the problem. We were cordially welcomed into the office where the meeting was to take place. There was a clear impression that they wanted this whole affair over and done with. So did we. But we told them in no uncertain terms, that we were appalled at what had happened and reminded them that our names were still on a police list at the airport. The gentleman handed us both an envelope and asked us if we would consider the contents to be a suitable apology from the airline. We both agreed that we were happy with the apology. The matter was closed, we took our leave and phoned the consulate with our good news. They had some good news for us too; we were off the list at the airport.

The night before the meeting, George and I had discussed the possibility of this happening, so we were prepared for it. The offer was a number of free flights with the airline, which had to be taken up within a 12-month period. That was acceptable to me, I told them, and George agreed too, but on one condition. 'Jesus, what is he at?' I thought. The condition was that the lady who dealt with us on the night of the altercation would not lose her job, as all she was doing was carrying out company policy. I was impressed, and I think they were too. They assured us that the lady in question would remain in her job, although we will never know if that is, in fact, what happened. The matter was closed and we took our leave and phoned the consulate with our good news.

Wednesday, 13 July saw us back in Los Angeles. Sadly, the Red Lion Hotel was booked out, and our last hotel base of the tournament was the Beverly Garland Hotel on Vineland Avenue, North Hollywood. This hotel was not on the official list of World Cup hotels, and I don't know how we finished up there, but I suspect that they knew there was no way we would agree to return to our downtown hotel. The hotel brochure informed us that Beverly Garland was a 'world-famous movie star'. She may well have been, but neither of us had ever heard of her. However, it was a fine hotel with a pool, and we were almost at the end of our travels.

It was an afternoon kick-off at the Rose Bowl where, once again, the Brazilians were finding it tough going against Sweden. With ten minutes remaining, Romario came to the rescue and the South Americans were into yet another World Cup final. On the other side of the United States, in Giants Stadium, Roberto Baggio scored twice for the Italians, which saw them book their place in the final. Sweden and Bulgaria would play for third and fourth places the following Saturday.

Despite the fact that this game is largely meaningless, 91,500 spectators turned up at the Rose Bowl. As a contest, it was all over at half-time as Sweden totally outplayed an exhausted Bulgaria, winning 4–0. The important thing for us was that the game did not go to extra time, or worse still, a penalty shootout. We needed to get back to the hotel as quickly as possible in order to get spruced up for the Three Tenors concert that night at the famous Dodger Stadium. This was an occasion not to be missed. Maurice Reidy flew up from Dallas to join us for the final. We were delighted to be able to tell him that there was a third ticket available for the concert.

The Concert

Dodger Stadium has been the venue for many impressive events. The Beatles performed there on their first-ever tour of the USA and the famous Simon and Garfunkel reunion concert was also held there. For the concert, it would have a capacity of 56,000, and ticket prices started at $15. The top-priced ticket was $1,000. We guarded our tickets with our lives as we made our way to the stadium. Our seats were in the VIP section of the stadium. As we looked around, it soon became apparent that we were among the 'great and the good'. George Bush Senior was directly behind us, Whoopie Goldberg was just to our right, and George spotted one of his heroes a few rows in front of us, the great Bob Hope. I was under orders there and then to take a photo of George with his idol. Hope was amazing.

'So you guys are from Ireland. I just got back from there a few days ago, my daughter has a house in Galway. Why don't you sit down, and we'll get someone to take a picture of the three of us. And look, there's Sinatra over there, you should get a picture taken with Frank.'

A few seats away, there was 'ol' blue eyes'. However, as we approached him, a dour-looking security man came between Sinatra and us, and the message was clear.

'Mr Sinatra ain't talkin' today.'

You win one, you lose one.

The concert was magnificent, not just because of the three main performers, but also because of The Los Angeles Philharmonic and the Los Angeles Music Centre Opera Chorus, all under the baton of Zubin Metha. The setting too was splendid. A stage that measured 60-yards wide was surrounded by two 48-feet high waterfalls, one on either side, which used 30,000 gallons of recycled water. All of this was framed by 20 classical columns, designed and constructed in Hungary, each column 40-feet high. Sound quality was superb. There were two huge screens which provided close-up shots of the performers, not that we needed them, as we were almost close enough to the performers to shake their hands.

Those of us in the VIP seats were provided with an information booklet, much of it interesting, some of it trivial. For example, the concert organisers informed us that 10,000 'Three Tenors' sandwich plates, 26,000 croissants, 20,000 fruit salads, 10,000 pasta dishes, 15,000 chocolate-dipped strawberries and 12,000 gallons of ice-cream would be eaten during the show that day. 15,000 bottles of water and 40,000 soft drinks would also be consumed.

It was exhilarating. We were glad to be part of an event watched on television by one billion people in 70 different countries around the world. We returned to the hotel in a good frame of mind to start packing for the trip home the next night. All we needed now was a good final the next day.

The Cockatoo in the Cab

The morning of the World Cup Final, 17 July, got off to a bizarre start. Maurice, George and I had decided not to avail of the media shuttle service, as we knew it would almost certainly be chaotic. The seating capacity for the press in the Rose Bowl was 1,389. 880 of these were provided with table tops, 509 were not. Add to that the vast numbers of television commentary teams who would be making their way to Pasadena for the game. We decided to pre-book a taxi and our man arrived on time, but not on his own. Sitting in a cage on the front seat was a large, white and very noisy cockatoo. The cab driver apologised profusely for the behaviour of his travelling companion and tried to explain the bird's presence.

'I gotta say I'm sorry for this mother-fucker of a bird, fellas. It's like this. I've had him in the car all mornin' drivin' downtown, but I gotta take the son-of-a-bitch to Pasadena, and you boys are the first chance I got to go out there. There's some old dame waitin' for this noisy bastard, and thanks to you boys she won't have to wait much longer.'

He was a tonic first thing in the morning. We jokingly asked him why he could not have made a quick trip to Pasadena to drop off the bird.

'Jeeeeesus boys, it's the day of the final and I gotta make a few bucks, and I can tell that you don't mind the bird being in the car. So tell me, is it going to be Brazil or Nigeria?'

Everyone had hoped that it would be a final worthy of the occasion, but that was not to be. It was tense, but with few scoring chances. After 120 goalless minutes, the World Cup final would be decided for the first time ever by penalty kicks. The Brazilians prevailed in the shootout, but there was great sympathy for Roberto Baggio, who missed the crucial penalty. Baggio had come to the rescue more than once during the course of the tournament. Without him, Italy would not have reached the final. Vice-President Al Gore presented the famed trophy to the Brazilian captain, Dunga, and brought the curtain down on USA 94.

The Post-Tournament Verdict

There were misgivings about the staging of the finals in America, but those misgivings proved to be unfounded. The event was regarded as a resounding success and broke all records for attendances. Just under 3·5 million spectators watched the 52 matches, an average of 65,000 per game. This broke the previous record attendance figure which had stood since 1950. There were a number of other firsts too. It was the first World Cup where players had their names on their jerseys. Russia competed for the first time as an independent state, following the dissolution of the Soviet Union. For the first time, three points were awarded for a win in the group stages to encourage more attacking play. This proved to be successful as during the course of the tournament there were 141 goals scored, which is an average of 2·7 goals per game.

From the perspective of the RTÉ commentary team, it certainly created a new record in terms of distances covered at a World Cup. George and I travelled on 21 flights and clocked up approximately 41,800 kilometres. As we waited to board our penultimate flight on the night of the final, we couldn't help but notice the rather large man who was being ushered into the lounge. It was Luciano Pavarotti, who was on the same British Airways flight to Heathrow Airport. This was too good an opportunity to miss. Almost instinctively, we both retrieved our concert tickets from the night before and asked the great man to sign them for us. He was more than happy to do so and even remarked on the fact that we had such very good tickets. We agreed that they were, indeed, very good tickets. Then it was time to head for home.

Two months after the World Cup, George handed me an article he had spotted in an English newspaper. It was a full-page story which dealt with the drug problem in downtown Los Angeles and the efforts that were being made to deal with the problem. The article was accompanied by a large photograph of the white igloo-type buildings which we could see clearly from our hotel rooms, just a few weeks before. The article was proof positive, if it were needed, that we had made the right decision in leaving that hotel.

George also came across a film which featured Beverly Garland, the 'world-famous film star'.

Almost a year later, I presented myself in the offices of American Airlines in Dublin, with the voucher that I had gladly accepted in San Francisco. The voucher was due to expire in a few weeks and, therefore, had to be used fairly quickly. The lady in the office inspected this document and offered her opinion.

'God, you must have really been insulted to have a voucher like this!'

I assured her that I had indeed been insulted.

Ossie Bennett and Tadhg in Ossie's pride and joy, his 1901 *De Dion Bouton* vintage car. For 40 years he took the car to the London–Brighton rally, one of the most famous vintage car rallies in the world. He took Tadhg along in 1999 – in this photo the pair are pictured on the outskirts of Brighton.

Ossie at the starting line in Hyde Park, London. The slower cars began the rally a little earlier, and the *De Dion* certainly qualified as part of that category. Note the long steel handle used for steering the car, not dissimilar to a tiller on a boat.

Road signs and banners you meet along the way. A colleague,
Tom Flanagan, took this photo of Tadhg outside Moneygall.

The Terminator and the Floor Manager. Guiding Arnie through the
crowds at the opening of Planet Hollywood. He asked Tadhg
to write out four words in Irish for him, '*Beidh mé ar ais*'.

Marty Morrissey interviews new Super Bantamweight boxing World
Champion Bernard Dunne at the 02 Arena, Dublin in March 2009.

During his tenure as GAA
President, Seán Kelly honoured
Tadhg with one of his
President's Awards in 1996. The
awards were presented by
Seán and then Taoiseach Bertie
Ahern at a banquet in Croke
Park.

The Memory Man and stalwart of RTÉ Sports broadcasting: Jimmy Magee presents his commentary from ringside at Bernard Dunne's victorious boxing match at which Dunne became the Super Bantamweight World Champion in March 2009. A very intent Joanne Cantwell, ringside reporter, is pictured beside him.

Floor Manager Don Irwin (left) puts the 'other' *Sunday Game* panel through their paces in Croke Park. This is the final check prior to transmission. On the panel are Eoin Byrne, sports administrator, John Dowdall, staging, and Sinéad O'Hanlon, who designed the set.

Thomond Park's redevelopment in 2008 has produced a state-of-the-art stadium. The photo above shows the calm before the storm in the new dressing room.

Tracy Piggott sings the national anthem along with the crowd in Thomond Park before the Munster v All Blacks match in November 2008.

The arrival of the match ball by helicopter on the night of the first match in refurbished Thomond Park in 2008 was not a first in Irish sport. My good friend in the Westmeath GAA County Board, Séamus Ó Faoláin, told me that when Cusack Memorial Park was officially opened in Mullingar on Sunday 16 July 1933, a plane flew in over the ground and the ball was thrown out the door as it passed over. Now that was style!

Five minutes to go against the All Blacks. Munster hooker Frankie Sheahan can hardly bear to watch on the historic opening night of the refurbished Thomond Park in November 2008.

Irish Rugby International Tommy Bowe gives a rendition of 'The Black Velvet Band' outside the Mansion House, Dublin March 2009 as the Irish rugby team enjoy a celebratory homecoming from Cardiff after winning their first Grand Slam since 1948.

Davy Fitzgerald, Waterford's hurling manager, decides this is the best time and place in which to hold a final team talk with his players prior to their match against Kilkenny in Croke Park, 2009.

He obviously failed to see or hear the Artane Boys' Band parading up the field towards him . . .

In the Croke Park tunnel with Paul McGinley and the Ryder Cup. Paul, an accomplished Gaelic footballer, was a special guest in Croke Park a few weeks after he holed the winning putt at the Ryder Cup in 2002.

The All-Ireland football final between Tyrone and Kerry in 2005. Note the gap in the Tyrone parade line. This was a mark of respect to the late team captain Cormac McAnallen.

Checking the running order with former GAA president Nicky Brennan at the Vodafone GAA All Stars awards ceremony, City West Hotel, 2008.

Tadhg, Tony Davis – *The Sunday Game* analyst – and commentator
Ger Canning in a relaxed mood in Croke Park.

This is the door into one of the warm-up rooms under the Hogan Stand
in Croke Park. The glass pane in the door is obviously not
designed to take the full force of a sliothar.

Jerry Grogan, Event Director in Croke Park. Calmness personified on big match days, except when Kerry are playing.

Martin McAleese, President Mary McAleese, Tadhg and his son Dara in Áras an Uachtaráin. Makes a change from meeting them in Croke Park!

Enough! 40 odd years as floor manager in RTÉ can leave a man on the ropes!

7
Madness in the Hotel

The Winners' Banquet

Ciaran McGeeney, Armagh's team captain, talked about the 'madness of the hotel' as he stood in the middle of Croke Park that Sunday evening of the 2002 All-Ireland football Final clash with Kerry. But he could not have known what to expect, as he had never had the experience of being in the winners' hotel on the night of a final. I could have told him what was ahead of him that night.

In the late 1980s, *The Sunday Game* brought a new dimension to RTÉ's Sunday night programme, when it paid a number of 'live' visits to the hotel where the winning team were attending their celebratory banquet. The first of these visits welcomed viewers to the hotel and promised interviews with members of the victorious team later in the programme.

After the match highlights were shown, Marty Morrissey and Ger Canning chatted with the winning captain and the manager of the team. A later visit usually involved Ger and Marty talking to one or two of the 'characters' on the team. The climax of the evening in the hotel involved the presentation of the 'man of the match' trophy.

The addition of the live broadcast from the winning hotel changed the complexion of the day considerably. Up to then, we would end our day in Croke Park with a number of interviews with members of the winning team. By 6.30 p.m. the working day was over. Going to the hotel changed all that.

The whereabouts of that hotel was not known until the referee blew his final whistle around 5 p.m. As soon as the match result became known, a small outside broadcast unit and crew would leave

Donnybrook and make their way to the appropriate hotel. For those of us at the match who had to make our way there later, the location of the hotel was very important indeed.

Some teams liked to stay well away from the city and the fans. They would choose a hotel such as The Grand Hotel in Malahide for their weekend stay. The Grand is a fine hotel, but Malahide was not where we wanted to go in the traffic after an All-Ireland final. The thought of the trip back into town at midnight ruled Malahide out as one of our favourite venues. For me, a hotel anywhere on the southside of the city was ideal, as it was on my way home. But county boards do not consider my travel arrangements when booking their hotel. The Burlington Hotel hosted many winning banquets, and it was well equipped to do so. Hosting a live programme in the banquet room was nothing new for the staff at the Burlington, as for many years it was the venue for the All-Stars dinner and the Highlights of the Year programme. Tipperary and Kerry took us to the Leopardstown Racecourse Complex on two occasions, while we also visited the Davenport, Jurys and The Green Isle.

Strong Men Needed Now!

These functions were usually run by the county associations which were based in Dublin. Initially they were attended by a few hundred guests. Without doubt, the most enjoyable ones were those where a team had won its very first All-Ireland or had won after an absence of many years. I recall an elated Brian McEniff, who guided Donegal to victory in 1992, being almost speechless that night when he realised the enormity of what he and his team had achieved. Brian and I enjoyed a good chat that night, and he reminded me that he was once my manager when I played the piano in his Bundoran hotel 25 years earlier.

Twelve months later, Derry made the breakthrough in 1993 when they came from nowhere to win their first All-Ireland. As the team arrived into the victory banquet that night, a member of the county board wept openly as he watched in disbelief. A few months earlier, I met this same man at an Ulster Championship match and I remarked to him that I was surprised at the relatively small turnout of Derry supporters. His explanation took me aback.

'The headbangers are marchin' today, and our people are at home mindin' their houses!'

The marching season was in full swing in the North.

The hurling final of 1994 was for me the five-minute final. Limerick people won't thank me for reminding them of it. Offaly went on a scoring spree in the dying minutes of the game, and Limerick lost a match that earlier they seemed certain to win. There were wild celebrations in the Offaly hotel that night, but it was a strange night for their manager Eamon Cregan. Eamon was an All-Ireland winner with his native Limerick in 1973. He knew what his fellow countymen were suffering in another hotel across the city that night. Ciaran Carey was a member of the Limerick team on that fateful day. He summed it up a few weeks later with a rather stark comment. He told me that 'there were no bushes in Croke Park'.

Ger Loughnane brought Clare to the final in 1995. The Banner County had 31 counties behind them in their quest for All-Ireland glory after suffering years of heartbreak. They spent 81 years in the wilderness, but after winning the Munster Final there was a huge belief around the team that 1995 would be their year. At half-time the game was still in the balance and a number of people spoke in the Clare dressing room during the interval, but not Loughnane. Just before the team took to the field for the second-half, Loughnane uttered four stimulating words.

'Strong men needed now!'

He left the dressing room and told Marty Morrissey in a brief interview on the sideline that Clare would win the game – of that he was certain.

The Clare team celebrated that famous win in the Davenport Hotel in the centre of Dublin that night. Driving to the hotel from Croke Park, it seemed that every Clare-registered car in the country was making its way to the venue. Supporters who had planned on returning home to the county after the game decided that this was a night they had to be with their heroes. The atmosphere was electric at the official dinner. Huge throngs of fans tried to talk their way into the banquet room. Loughnane was hailed as the new messiah, and the guests raised the roof when he took exception to a remark made by Eamon Cregan who was on *The Sunday Game* panel in Donnybrook. Cregan, a former Limerick player and ex-Offaly manager, said the final had been a poor game of hurling. I had suggested to Ger that he might ignore it as Clare had proved that they were now the best team in the country, but that's not the way Ger works. He couldn't let it go unanswered, and the crowd loved it.

Man of the Match Award

For those of us who started the day in Croke Park at 9.30 a.m., the final act of the day is a welcome relief 14 hours later. This is the announcement and presentation of the 'Man of the Match' award. Sometimes this can be a straightforward affair when the player in question is a clear winner and there is unanimous approval of the selection from all sides. However, when four or five players are in contention for this prestigious award, those attending the winners' banquet see it as a challenge to find out who the winner is before the announcement is made. There are a number of ways to elicit this information from an unsuspecting floor manager as he chases around the room setting up interviews.

'Jaysus, RTÉ, how could ye give man of the match to Jamesie. Sure Lohan had a blinder.'

You have to give credit where it's due, but that's a classic example of a triple whammy. In reply, you can't say that Jamesie did not win the award, as that would take him out of the equation, and which one of the two Lohan brothers had a 'blinder'? Usually, I complimented the questioner and gave him good marks for effort, pointing out that we still had not been told who was the actual winner. This was often true, and I always preferred not knowing who the 'man of the match' was until as late as possible. I have to pay tribute to two Corkmen who were desperate to find out who had won the award at a victory dinner a few years ago. They had a novel approach.

'We're from Joe Deane's club, and we were wonderin' would you bring Joe over to our table for a photograph when he gets the man of the match?'

On that same night, we had planned on interviewing Ben O'Connor, one of the two identical twins. I know Ben and Jerry for a few years now but still can't tell one from the other, and I was determined not to mix them up on that occasion and feel like a fool again. Before approaching Ben, I asked Con Murphy, the Cork team doctor, to guide me in the right direction.

'Tadhg, you're long enough around now to know the O'Connors. That's Ben on the left and Jerry is over there.'

I rambled confidently across to Ben and told him that we would like to interview him during the course of the evening.

'Tadhg boy, you've done it again! I'm Jerry!'

I'm not sure if Con set me up that night, and if he did I hope he enjoyed it. He has given loyal service to Cork teams down the years. His first visit to Croke Park with a Cork side was in 1957, when he was the team mascot at the All-Ireland final.

The nightmare scenario at the 'man of the match' presentation is that the man in question goes missing, and it has happened. It's a closely guarded secret up to the last moment, but camera operators need to know where the winner is sitting before the announcement is made.

Before the end of the meal I stand briefly behind the winner's chair to identify his location in the banquet room. Let me hasten to add this system will be changed in the future. It's a heart-stopping moment to discover that the chair which was occupied by the man of the match-to-be has been vacated and 'our man' is suddenly nowhere to be seen.

Some players never consider themselves as candidates for the award. When dinner ends, they often leave to join up with friends out in one of the many packed bars in the hotel. On the night that Tyrone won their second final in 2005, Owen Mulligan was chosen as man of the match. In order to keep him in his seat, I had told him that Marty would interview him at the table during the programme. Near the end of the programme, Mulligan decided that we had forgotten all about him, so he wandered out to the hotel lobby. The announcement was only one minute away when I found him and bundled him, unceremoniously and without explanation, back into his chair. Owen was totally shocked, as he certainly did not expect to be named 'man of the match'. He was clearly embarrassed by it all and protested that he did not deserve the award.

A Big Galway Rabbit

There was no such embarrassment at the Wexford hurlers' winning celebrations in 1996. The county had been starved of success since 1968. It was great to see Martin Storey and George O'Connor enjoy the taste of victory. At the end of games in Croke Park, Martin would 'borrow' a cigarette from me and enjoy a quiet smoke in the tunnel before returning to the dressing room. He was not the only one.

Bobby Ryan, Tipperary captain in 1989, 'borrowed' many a cigarette in that same tunnel at the end of a game. Bobby was a character, and a few days before that final Jimmy Magee visited the Ryan family home to talk to Bobby about the game. After the game the following Sunday, Jimmy chatted to Bobby again on the radio and thanked him and his family for their hospitality during the week. He did not expect the reply he got.

'Do ye know Jimmy, we thought you were goin' to eat us out of house and home!'

Returning to the Wexford victory of 1996, I recall a lovely moment which happened on the morning of their semi-final victory over Galway. Many people had expected Galway to win that game, and one of their star players that day was the great Joe Rabbitte. On the way to Croke Park, I noticed a few Wexfordmen parked at the East Link toll bridge. They had obviously decided to travel to Dublin early and were enjoying sandwiches and flasks of tea as they sat on the banks of the Liffey. Three of them were fishing. Another carload of Wexfordmen pulled up beside the anglers and the conversation went as follows;

'There's the men. Any luck, boys?'

'Not a bite so far anyway, but we're only here a few minutes.'

'Fair play to ye. What kind of fish would ye get here?'

'We'd be hopin' for an old mullet or two, maybe.'

'And what kind of bait are ye usin' there?'

'Ah sure there's only one kind of bait to be usin' on a day like today – a big fuckin' Galway rabbit!'

Having to Lick a Corkman's Arse

The streets around the Burlington Hotel were thronged with Galway supporters on the night of the 1998 football final. The hotel had closed its doors early in the night, and for a very good reason. It was packed to capacity with celebrating fans who were fortunate enough to get in early, hoping to catch a glimpse of their heroes. It was 32 years since the county last won a final, and the Burlington Hotel had never witnessed anything like the party that took place all through the night. John Glynn, a Galway man himself, was general manager of the hotel at the time and at 4 a.m. he had to order a fleet of taxis to ferry in extra supplies of beer and stout – the hotel's bars had run dry.

Seán Ó Domhnaill scored a great point for Galway in that final from about 40 yards from goal (folklore has stretched this distance and it is now said that he was at least 70 yards from goal). Ó Domhnaill raised both hands in the air to celebrate the score and was reprimanded by team captain, Ray Silke, who reminded him that the match was far from won. The Carraroe man told Silke that he appreciated the match was far from over but that it would look good on the video at Christmas.

You may be surprised that I haven't mentioned any of Kerry's victorious nights and how they celebrate them. It's a very special night for the team and panel of players, but for the guests attending the function it's just another Kerry All-Ireland night. They turn up, have the dinner, listen to the speeches, watch the television interviews, cheer on the 'man of the match' winner and take 'Sam' home with them. Job done.

Kilkenny are somewhat similar. They take it all in their stride. During a commercial break in *The Sunday Game* a few years ago, I told the audience in the hotel that we had received phone calls from viewers saying that the atmosphere at the winners' function was very subdued. The audience suggested that Michael Lyster inform the viewers that Kilkenny people were used to these occasions and would not get overly excited.

In 2000, Millennium year, people in Kilkenny did get excited. To honour the arrival of the new century, two teams of the century were chosen in hurling and football. Special postage stamps were issued to commemorate the teams and individual players' portraits appeared on the stamps. There was utter dismay in Kilkenny when the hurling team was announced. Ray Cummins from Cork was chosen at full-forward instead of one of Kilkenny's legends, DJ Carey.

Barrie Enrique of the *Kilkenny People* told me of the reaction of one supporter in the county when the news broke. 'How could those selectors leave a player like DJ Carey off that team? One of the greatest hurlers of all time, and they put Ray Cummins ahead of him. That's just adding insult to injury because now, every time I want to post a letter, I have to lick a Corkman's arse!'

Triumph Tinged with Tragedy

In 2003, Peter Canavan took possession of 'Sam' and carried it into a thronged Burlington Hotel, which was bathed in a sea of red and white. Earlier in the afternoon, I witnessed an extraordinary scene in the Tyrone dressing room, as the team and officials gathered around the famous trophy which they had just won for the first time and sang the National Anthem.

They returned two years later to win a second time but that celebration was tinged with sadness. Cormac McAnallen, the team captain, had died suddenly in the intervening year. His tragic loss motivated the team to strive for that success in the absence of their friend and teammate. There was a very poignant moment in Croke Park that afternoon during the team parade. The Tyrone men left a gap in the parade as they marched around the stadium. The empty space was where Cormac would have been had he not passed away so suddenly, and at such a young age.

That night in the hotel, I got a great insight into the leadership qualities of Mickey Harte off the field. As the team lined up waiting to be ushered into the banqueting hall, Mickey addressed his troops.

'Now boys, we didn't buy you those jackets to hang them on the back of a chair, so would you all put them on, please. Put down your drinks, boys, the only thing we are carrying into that room with us is the Sam Maguire.'

Two weeks earlier, Cork had won the hurling final and team captain Seán Óg Ó hAilpín will always be remembered for his stirring speech after the game. Seán made another speech that night at the victory dinner, which was received with enthusiasm by the Cork supporters. It was another superb speech, in English and Irish, but I remember it best for the request he made as he ended. He told the large gathering that he hoped they would all savour the victory that night and the return journey to Cork the next day – and he finished by asking everybody to drink sensibly.

The day had been a personal triumph for Seán Óg, yet here he was urging his fellow countymen and women to take care of themselves on the way home. He is, without doubt, a wonderful person, as well as being an outstanding athlete. Later that night, he put on his training shoes and went for a run.

Tragedy visited the Kilkenny hurlers in 2008 with the tragic death of Vanessa McGarry, wife of James, the sub goalkeeper. Henry Shefflin, the Kilkenny captain, will be long remembered for his wonderful gesture on the steps of the Hogan Stand when he invited Vanessa's son, Darragh, to accept the All-Ireland trophy with him after the county's victory. Later that night at the victory celebrations, young Darragh was surrounded by members of the Kilkenny team. The team members wore their specially tailored suits and young Darragh was dressed in the same attire as the team. It was all very poignant, and it became very clear that the team were totally dedicated to winning that game for Vanessa. It was a huge motivating factor. Talking to the players that night I began to realise that Limerick were probably unaware of the mountain they had to climb that day. There was an air of quiet satisfaction in the Kilkenny hotel that night. Job done.

All victory nights have that air about them, the feeling of 'a job done'. Players get together with their families to celebrate a great achievement. The tensions of the weeks prior to the game have suddenly disappeared, and the pressure on the team and management has lifted.

Two thousand Armagh supporters sat down to dinner in the City

West Hotel on the night Ciaran McGeeney lifted the Sam Maguire cup in Croke Park. The 'Sam' sat proudly at the top table, but I borrowed it to place it on a plinth in our presentation area for the first of our live transmission for *The Sunday Game*. As I made my way up through the packed diners, a man jumped up from his seat and asked me could he take a photograph of the cup and touch it, just for a moment. I told him that I had a better idea – I'd take a photo of him with the cup. His wife joined him, and they cradled the cup as I took the picture. They were dizzy with excitement. Over an hour later, as I returned the cup to the top table, the man again approached me and pushed a €50 note into my pocket. He said he could never thank me enough and wanted the RTÉ lads to have a drink on him. He could not understand why I would not accept his generosity, and I had to put the money on the floor and walk away. That's what it meant to him to have that picture.

And that's the 'madness of the hotel' on All Ireland nights. Players get together with friends and family to celebrate a great achievement. The tension in the weeks prior to the game has lifted. Job done. All the pressure is off, and the journey home next day is still to come.

8
Memories of Lansdowne Road

The Oldest Rugby Ground in the World

Iwas in Ballsbridge in 2007, a few weeks after the last game was played in Lansdowne Road, and I took a small detour out of curiosity. The stadium was being demolished and I wanted to see how the wrecking crew was getting on. Turning the corner off Shelbourne Road, I realised that I had left it late to get a final glimpse of the old ground. Dublin's other great sporting venue, a landmark on the southern side of the Liffey, was gone.

The demolition team had done their work well and with amazing speed. Standing at the railway level-crossing, I was shocked to see the famous 16-acre site had been levelled to the ground. The West Stand, which housed the RTÉ commentary box, wasn't there anymore. Havelock Square terrace was flattened, and the South Terrace, atop of which the RTÉ studio was once located, was a pile of rubble.

Rising from the dust, the giant pillars of the new West Stand were already growing tall – a clear indication that the 'new' Lansdowne Road stadium was fast becoming a reality. But the oldest international rugby venue in the world was gone. Though it had long since passed its sell-by date, it made me sad.

Henry William Doveton Dunlop was the man who had the vision to start it all. He founded Lansdowne Rugby Club in 1872. He was also a very accomplished athlete and wanted to create a sporting arena in Dublin. He purchased a 21-year lease on the grounds from Pembroke Estate and founded the Irish Champion Athletic Club. The club went on to raise £1,000 which enabled them to level the ground, lay a running track and build a pavilion. The first-ever international athletic meet was held there in 1875, when Ireland took on England. However, the ground was considered unsuitable for the first rugby international between Ireland and England, and the game was played at the Leinster Cricket ground in Rathmines.

In 1878, Ireland met England again at international level and the game was played at Lansdowne Road on 11 March. Up to the time of its demolition, all of Ireland's senior international rugby matches were played at the famous ground. The Irish Rugby Football Union eventually acquired the lease, which had been sold by Doveton. The Dublin 4 ground flourished and became one of the most famous rugby venues in the world.

But now it's gone and will be replaced by a new state-of-the-art stadium, which will meet the demands of the modern age. This, of course, is as it should be, but I will always have fond memories of the old ground and my time there. There's a particularly bad memory too – a night when English soccer 'fans' came to Dublin to stop a football game and succeeded.

I had to wait a few years before I got to work in Lansdowne Road. In my early years as a floor manager, my position in the pecking order was well down the line and there was little chance of getting to work on the Five Nations championship, as it was known then. The more senior floor managers at the time regarded Lansdowne Road as the place to be on international days. So I saw the game on television or watched from the terrace. Even then, there was a certain 'aura' about rugby in Ireland, and it was still perceived as an elitist game. Having played the game in school, I could never understand that mentality but it existed.

RTÉ's Rugby Coverage in the Early Years

Coverage of rugby matches was pretty basic in the early years of RTÉ, as it was with other sports. There was no studio at the ground, and no pre-match panel discussion or interviews with the managers prior to the game. Fred Cogley welcomed viewers a few minutes before kick-off, and at the end of the game there was a scrambled interview on the touchline with a coach or player, who invariably got mobbed by supporters. There was no half-time discussion with a panel of experts, or a look at the scores or incidents from the first-half. All rugby internationals now have a 15-minute break at half-time, and both teams go to their dressing rooms. But it used to be different. In the early television years, the teams remained on the field, and two boys would bring two trays of orange slices onto the pitch. The oranges were devoured in no time, and the sides turned around in a few minutes and got on with the business in hand.

Because of the proximity of Jury's Hotel to Lansdowne Road, RTÉ has used it on a regular basis to host a lunch for visiting commentators or sports producers from other broadcasting organisations. Clive Woodward, the former England and Lions manager, attended one of these lunches and he told me a wonderful story concerning those short half-time breaks from his playing days with England.

It concerned a Five Nations international match between Ireland and England, which was being played at Twickenham. One of the English players was a diabetic, and it was arranged that at half-time a young lad would bring out a plate with a few lumps of sugar to this player. However, the excitement of the occasion was too much for the youngster. He panicked and couldn't remember which player he was meant to give the sugar to. The nearest player to him was the legendary Moss Keane.

'Excuse me sir, are you the gentleman for the sugar?' he inquired timidly.

The young lad had great difficulty understanding the significance of the heaving breathless reply given in Moss's trademark Kerry accent.

'Who the fuck do ye think I am . . . Nijinsky?'

136

Woodward was only a few feet away from this incident, and he still remembers it vividly.

Back to Lansdowne Road. Nowadays we take for granted the television build-up to the Six Nations games and the post-match analysis with slow-motion replays from four different camera angles. Team managers and players are interviewed, always in front of the mandatory backdrop which bears the logos of the various sponsors of the tournament. All post-match interviews must be conducted in front of this backdrop.

The TV interview area is a chaotic place to be after a Six Nations match, with up to five or six backdrops belonging to the various television channels. Everybody wants the interview *now*. Just as importantly, everybody wants the interview first. There's a pecking order for post-match interviews on Six Nations match days, with the host broadcaster having priority and the home broadcaster next in line.

The BBC are the host broadcaster, even in Ireland, and I have had a great working relationship with my floor manager colleague from the 'Beeb'. When the Irish manager and captain are brought in, we arrange that one or other of them will talk to RTÉ and the BBC first, and then we simply swap them around when they finish. It's a good local arrangement and it ensures that both stations have two interviews within minutes of the match ending. The manager and captain will then give interviews to the other networks which have access to the TV room, such as BBC Northern Ireland, BBC Wales, BBC Scotland and S4C, the Welsh language station.

It was through S4C that I first met the great Welsh legend Ray Gravelle, who worked for the station after his illustrious career in the Welsh jersey came to an end. We became good friends and Ray would always promise me on match days that he would bring one of the Welsh team over to me when he was finished with them. He was always as good as his word, but Ray's interviews went on for anything up to ten minutes and RTÉ were long off the air by the time he arrived with a player or two. His early passing was sad and he is sorely missed on match days.

The Post-Match Interviews

IRFU official Harry Booker paved the way for the post-match interviews under the stand in Lansdowne Road. He was a wonderful man and seemed to run Lansdowne Road on his own. If we had a problem on match day, we went to Harry and he solved it in his own quiet way.

In 1982, Harry really pushed out the boat for RTÉ. Up to that year the only after-match interview was the pitch-side interview – one which was usually conducted in the middle of a mass of supporters. 1982 was to change all that. Ireland were due to play Scotland and victory in that game would mean a first Triple Crown in over 30 years. RTÉ wanted to extend its coverage for the big occasion and requested permission to put a camera underneath the West Stand close to the dressing-room corridor.

In the event of an Irish victory, we would then be able to do a good number of post-match interviews in relative peace. However, this location was 'off-limits' to all except IRFU officials and invited dignitaries. It was unthinkable that television 'riff-raff' would be allowed inside these hallowed walls.

Harry Booker came up with the solution. He decided not to bring the RTÉ request to the IRFU officials, as he knew it would most likely be turned down. Instead, he told us to put the camera and the microphone in place and to cover all the equipment with a tarpaulin so that it wouldn't attract too much attention. If Ireland won the game and the Triple Crown, then we could go ahead with the interviews and, hopefully, nobody would pay too much notice.

And that's exactly what did happen. Olly Campbell kicked six penalties and a drop goal and Ireland beat Scotland 21–12 to win the Triple Crown. We did our interviews after the game and everyone thought it was a great idea, and wondered why we hadn't done it before. All post-match interviews were conducted there after 1982. It was a wonderful afternoon and was only bettered three years later when Ireland won the Triple Crown again. The 1985 victory will always be remembered for Ciaran Fitzgerald calling for one final effort from his players in the closing, dramatic minutes of that game against England.

'Where's ye'er fucking pride?'

I heard it clearly from the touchline, and thousands of television viewers heard it all around the country. The response was almost instant. Donal Lenihan powered his way inside the English '22', and the ball eventually came back to Michael Kiernan. Kiernan had no choice. A dropped goal was on and he had to go for it. Time was almost up. Fifty thousand souls held their breaths as the ball sailed through the air on its way to the goalposts and over the bar. The place erupted. In sporting terms, it doesn't get much better than that. Moments later, the pitch was invaded and Fitzgerald and his team were engulfed in a sea of delirious supporters.

The legendary Mick Doyle was the Irish manager on that day. But for the help of two anonymous members of the Garda Síochána, I don't think I could have got Mick to the interview area. I have another great memory of Mick, this one from another Five Nations game during his tenure in charge. He brought the Irish forwards to Lansdowne Road around midday on the day of the game for some final lineout practice. As they went through their routines on the pitch, an over-zealous official told Mick that he would have to take them out onto the back pitch and finish the session there. Mick's reaction was instant.

'If you insist that I have to take my players out to the back pitch on the day of an international, I can tell you now there won't be a match at three o'clock.'

The players continued with their routine, and that was the end of it. It was the only time I ever saw Mick Doyle in a fit of rage, and he really meant his threat. That famous victory in 1985 was one of his greatest days, and it was achieved with a relatively new group of players whom he had brought into the side. It was, without doubt, one of the great days at the Ballsbridge venue. But there were some bad days too.

The Riot at Lansdowne Road

The Irish soccer team enthralled the nation with its exploits when it qualified for the European Championships for the first time in 1988. Two years later the team made it to the quarter-finals of the World Cup in Italy, and in 1994, Ireland qualified for a second World Cup, this time in the United States.

These were heady days for Irish soccer under Jack Charlton. The Euro 96 finals were to be held in England. It was the fervent wish of every Irish citizen that we would make it to these finals. Charlton was determined to take his team to his country of origin for a major championship. Ireland had played England in Lansdowne Road a few years earlier when both nations were drawn in the same group in the Euro qualifiers. The occasion passed off without incident, so when it was announced that the two countries would meet for a friendly game in Lansdowne Road, there was an instant clamour for tickets. The game would be a welcome challenge for the Irish in the build-up to qualification for Euro 96. Newly-appointed England manager Terry Venables looked forward to sending out his side against his fellow countryman and World Cup winner, Charlton.

It was a cold, crisp, dry night in Lansdowne when the two teams came out onto the pitch – ideal for a game of football. The atmosphere was electric and mostly good-humoured. The 2,000 or so English supporters were housed in the West Stand upper and lower decks, at the Wanderers' Pavilion end. They were raucous and loud, but did not seem to pose any threat to the enjoyment of the occasion. Earlier in the city centre, there had been some minor scuffles involving English fans, but there was no hint of trouble as the crowd settled down for what we all hoped would be a really good game.

It started off at a furious pace, and it was clear that both sides were truly up for it. Neither side wanted to lose this one. Here were two sides whose players battled against each other in various clubs in the Premier League, week in week out. Bragging rights were at stake here when they returned to their respective clubs. Twenty-two minutes into the game the stadium erupted. After a great run out of his own half by Terry Phelan, David Kelly put the ball past goalkeeper David Seaman and Ireland took the lead. The crowd went wild. This was what everyone had hoped for. Memories of Stuttgart came flooding back.

Three minutes later, a collective groan echoed around the ground when David Platt scored for England but the linesman had his flag raised as Alan Shearer was clearly offside. Exactly one minute later, as the Irish were on the offensive again, a crescendo of booing started around the ground, and it grew steadily in volume. Ger Canning and I were standing next to the Irish dugout and we both wondered why the crowd was booing. There was nothing happening on the field that would have merited such booing. The noise level was increasing all the time. I can clearly recall Paul Ince and Warren Barton looking up to the West Stand with a look of dismay on both their faces. Then I heard George Hamilton on my headphones.

'There's trouble in the stand!'

The trouble was to our right and behind us. Many of the players were by now looking up into the West Stand, many of them with a look of dismay on their faces. Large pieces of timber were being thrown down from the upper deck, and many of them were landing among the fans in the lower deck. It made no sense. These thugs were throwing lethal missiles (bits of seats) down on their own fellow countrymen, women and children. It was beyond belief.

The referee made up his mind very quickly and ordered the players off the pitch and into the safety of the dressing rooms. The spectators in the lower tier of the stand started to spill out onto the field to avoid being struck by lethal missiles from above. Ray Treacy was the co-commentator with George Hamilton, and he tried to allay the fears of those watching the unfolding mayhem at home on television. Ray said that it was important to note that the trouble was coming from the English section, and that it had been cordoned off. He assured viewers that there were no Irish supporters in that section. George agreed with the decision made by the referee to take the players off the field and voiced his anger at what was happening.

'This is a disgrace. It is a scandal. It should never have happened and the people in the West Upper Stand throwing the missiles do not deserve to be here, or indeed, in any football stadium. Sadly, English football has attracted, in its wake, this kind of support. They have caused problems at home. They have caused problems abroad, and they are now causing problems in Lansdowne Road.'

Ray made the point that the ticket allocation for the English would have gone through the travelling supporters' club and that these thugs should be known to the authorities. The Irish fans in the sections next to the trouble areas left their seats in droves and made their way out onto the pitch and to safety. Within minutes, there were thousands on the field and the big question now was would the game have to be abandoned. It quickly became apparent that we were no longer covering a football match, but a major news story which would be viewed all around the world. I tried to get an interview with the referee, but not surprisingly he made it very clear that he would not be making any comment. No one seemed to know what was going on. The public address announcer asked people to stay calm.

By now, the troubled area was completely surrounded. The known thugs were being hauled out by baton-wielding members of the Gardaí.

I recall a bangharda wading into the area and dragging one of the hooligans down the touchline. To this day, I have no idea who she was but I was proud of her. I went down to have a closer look at the corner of the stand where the trouble was, and I have one frightening memory of it. You could see the bits of timber coming down from above in the floodlights, but what one could not see were the iron bolts, which held the seats together. You could only hear the thud as they landed on the pitch. George was right; these people should not be allowed into a game, anywhere.

The referee came back out on to the field to see the situation for himself, first-hand. With him were Paddy Daly, the FAI referee liaison officer, Supt Pat Doocey of the Garda Síochána and a number of security officials. Opinions were divided as to whether the match should continue. The public address told the crowd that the game had been called off but, in fact, no decision had yet been made at that time. I was with those officials on pitch-side and they returned to the dressing room still undecided.

I have no doubt that, at that point, the referee had no intention of restarting the game. Ger Canning did a live report from pitch-side, in which he gave a first-hand report from the trouble area. In it he described some of the missiles which we had seen coming from the upper deck – stones, coins, umbrellas and pieces of timber.

Bill O'Herlihy was back in the studio with Joe Kinnear and John Giles, and he asked Ger if anyone had been injured. He pointed out that many viewers had family members who were attending the game and would be concerned for their safety. Bill's daughter was at the game and he was worried. Ger told him that apart from one press photographer, there were no other reports of injuries. There were a good number of blood-spattered thugs being marched out of the stadium by the Gardaí, but they had 'run into' garda batons.

We did have a major concern for one of our colleagues, cameraman

Ben Eglinton, son of Tommy, a former Irish international. Ben was operating a camera which was directly in front of the English fans in the Upper West Stand. When the trouble broke out, he was isolated. His only way out was through the hostile crowd, and there was no way for anyone to get to him. Ben did the only thing he could. He pointed the camera at the ground, sat down and waited for deliverance. When the riot police got to the upper deck and a certain degree of calm was restored, Ben climbed over the stand rail and made his escape, much to our relief. It should be said that one of the English fans helped him out of the camera box and over the rail.

Under the West Stand in the interview area, the scene was chaotic. We pushed our way into a corner and managed to get Seán Connolly, then Chief Executive of the FAI, to do an interview. Ger Canning put it to him that the FAI would have to shoulder the blame for what had happened. Seán said that he was not so sure that was the case, and that the FAI had taken security advice regarding the positioning of the English. The inquiry into what went wrong would start immediately, he replied.

Graham Kelly, the English FA boss, was interviewed by Ger a few minutes later. Kelly said that he could not understand the kind of people who could show such callous disregard for the lives of children and other spectators. Ger told him that we thought the football hooligan problem had gone away, but clearly it had not. With respect, Kelly replied, people in Ireland might have thought that, but no one in England did. Because of good policing and good intelligence work, it was under control, but people who do this sort of thing simply don't go away. Kelly was asked how some of these fans got tickets, and he said he did not know, but that he had a lot of questions that needed answers.

Did he have any questions to ask the Football Association of Ireland?

No, he did not.

144

Then he was happy with the ticketing arrangements for tonight's game?

Yes, he was.

But surely, Ger insisted, the English fans should not have been put into that part of the ground. Kelly said that he could not say whether the fans were in the right part of the ground or not, and that the FA would carry out their own investigation.

Jack's Post-Riot Interview

Now we needed to talk to Jack Charlton. The huge viewing audience would want to hear what he had to say about the events of the night. Shortly after the match had been called off, I had spotted him out on the pitch, surrounded by policemen. He was in a rage. A young Irish fan had thrown something into the crowd, and Jack saw him do it. He did not want the Irish to retaliate in any way, so he roared at the culprit.

'Go home. It's over. Go home. Go home. Go home.'

He was infuriated, and I knew that asking Jack for an interview at that moment would not be a wise decision. However, the Minister for Sport, Bernard Allen, and Bertie Ahern, who was Leader of the Opposition at the time, were out on the side of the pitch. Both agreed to do an interview with Ger. They both castigated the English FA and asked how was it that these so-called 'fans' could get tickets for a match like this. The Minister said he accepted that this was a 'home game' for the Irish, but that he couldn't understand how so many English supporters could get into one corner of the ground and disrupt such a major sporting event. He also said that the English know the record of their fans, and the seating arrangements should have been better organised. Bertie Ahern said some English officials in the Presidential box had told him before the game that they recognised some of the visiting thugs. They were known to them.

Back in the studio, Bill O'Herlihy said he was astounded to hear that National Front supporters were identified by English officials before the game, yet nothing was done about it. Joe Kinnear disagreed with both politicians and said that no matter how enraged we were about what happened, the ball lay firmly in the court of the FAI. John Giles shared this view.

Ger interviewed a clearly shocked Terry Venables. He asked him what was his reaction to the game being abandoned because of these fans. Venables said that these were not fans, and that he simply could not understand these people. A few of his players came out to see the situation for themselves and were clearly embarrassed by what they saw. Their 'supporters', were still corralled in the stand, surrounded by a cordon of riot police. The atmosphere was strangely eerie, with the noise of barking police dogs ringing around the ground.

Jack regained his composure eventually, and we knew he was now ready to talk to us. He was asked for his reaction to the series of events.

'I'm very pleased with it all. You must be kidding! How can you ask a question like that? It was an absolute disaster – we don't experience things like that in Ireland. I feel ashamed at the whole business. I don't know what to say. The game was lovely, everyone was enjoying it, good competition. We scored a goal, the Irish were happy, it was a lovely game. Nobody had made a bad tackle in the game, everybody working hard. Then all of a sudden, whatever happened I don't know, my attention was drawn to the crowd. It appeared to me that the England supporters in the top deck were bombardin' the English in the bottom deck. I don't understand that. Throw them at the Irish if you want, but not at your own. I don't want to talk about it. I'm so mixed up and so sick of the whole business. It was a smashin' game – it's about football, innit? A whole nation is going to suffer because 2,000 lunatics were mixed in with 2,000 supporters. It's crazy, absolutely crazy. I just know that the game was abandoned because of aggravation in the corner of a football field. I've never seen a game called off because of that situation. We are now going to be involved in a long hard tussle about whose fault it was, and where, and what repercussions there are, and there will be many. That's why you're all stood here like this wanting stories. You've got loads of stories. You'll love it for the next fortnight, you'll have a ball.'

Ger asked Jack if he thought there might be implications for Euro 96.

'I've no idea. Not as far as we're concerned. We play the North here, and I guarantee you when they come down they'll behave themselves. And we will behave ourselves. There'll be none of that with us. Never has been. Every Englishman should be ashamed of what went on here tonight.'

He was angry, and he was ashamed too – we could sense it. The press conference lasted only a few minutes, and then he was gone. Things had calmed down considerably in the ground by the time we finished. It was almost midnight and Lansdowne Road was almost empty. The English fans had already been escorted from the stand, but the floodlights were still on, as the Gardaí searched through the debris. Before I left, I went to the upper deck of the West Stand to see for myself what these fans had left behind them. Seats had been smashed to pieces and long shards of timber with jagged edges littered the area. Missiles like these had been thrown down a few hours earlier. It was truly a miracle that no one was killed. I found a snooker ball among the debris.

And so ended the night of the 'friendly' against England, a sad night for sport in Ireland, a sad night for Lansdowne Road. The mindless violence we witnessed that night was new to followers of sport here. Most people had only seen this kind of thuggery on television and were deeply shocked when they witnessed it first-hand on our own doorstep.

9
Characters You Meet on the Road

Groundsmen & Carpark Attendants

One of the most rewarding aspects of being involved in television coverage of various sporting events is the number of characters you meet and the new friendships you strike up over a long period of time. In 40 years on the road covering sport, I have got to know the most amazing collection of individuals on this island.

The most obvious group among these people is those who run the various sporting organisations, both at local and national levels. However, the net stretches much wider than that. Team managers and their backroom staff, public relations people and in more recent years the media relations representative appointed by many teams to keep the heat off the manager. But there were others, just as important, whom you needed to know, or get to know, in order to make life a little easier.

High on this list was the man in charge of the carpark inside the ground. The power wielded by this individual was enormous, and he knew it. In his 'Locker Room' column in *The Irish Times*, sports journalist Tom Humphreys wrote that the carpark attendant at St Tiernach's Park in Clones would prefer if Tom parked his car in Finglas on match days! I understand exactly where Tom is coming from when he makes that observation.

Then there's the man on the turnstile, who has been given very clear instructions that nobody goes past him without the magic 'pass'. This can be a problem when you discover that you left your pass on the kitchen table at 7.30 a.m. Worse still is turning up with the magic document firmly clasped in your fist, only to be told you're at the wrong gate and invariably the gate you should be at was at the opposite end of the ground. There was a famous gate man in Croke Park in the early 1970s who refused admission to Mícheál O'Hehir on All-Ireland Final day because he didn't have his pass.

For me, the easiest way to overcome these obstacles was to get to know the people involved. While there was ample evidence around the country that there were some awkward and less-than-helpful individuals at various venues, I worked on the premise that most stewards, gate men and carpark officials were decent, run-of-the-mill people who were doing a job at these events – just like I was.

A few years ago I jokingly asked the carpark man at the Brandywell in Derry if my car would be safe. The reply was instant.

'This is the safest fuckin' place in Ireland. We don't even let the police in here!'

On another night in the Brandywell, I had a strange experience. A man whom I'd got to know at the ground down through the years asked me if I'd brought much sterling with me on my trip north. I was puzzled by the question. He explained that there was a house not too far away, and that if I went there with STG£300, I would be given STG£1,000 in return. This happened not too long after the infamous Northern Bank robbery, and I was assured that there was no catch and that everything was above board! I didn't take up the offer, or should I say I chickened out. I never did find out if this offer was for real. These were the kind of characters I loved to meet on the road and there was an abundance of them.

The Cornerboy in Thurles

Every town and village in Ireland has a 'cornerboy'. He's the one who spends long hours each day leaning against a building in the centre of that town or village watching the world go by. In his local pub at night, he can tell you the movements of the entire town, who went where and when. He prides himself on this knowledge, as if he were keeping a watchful eye on all the inhabitants of the town. A Wexfordman told me how to instantly recognise a 'cornerboy'. He claimed that the shoulders of the cornerboy's jacket were always shiny – from leaning up against walls!

During the years of the 'Emergency' – the early days of the Second World War – the Irish government established the LDF (Local Defence Force) to protect Ireland from any marauding German invaders. There were two cornerboys in a small midlands village and one of them decided to join up. It was not that he felt he had a duty to protect the nation, but more a case of availing of the free pair of boots and a warm military coat which came with being an LDF member. So he duly became a member and was given his new boots which, unfortunately, were at least four sizes too big for him. A few days later, he was walking down through the village and his pal was on duty, holding up the local corner shop.

'How's it goin' dere Mickey. Where are ya off to wit yer shiny new boots?' he shouted across the street.

The new recruit fired back, 'I'm goin' down to de end of de street to turn!'

On the Thursday before the 1991 hurling final we were in Liberty Square in Thurles recording 'vox pop' interviews, as they are known in television speak. The plan was to doorstep people as they went about their business and ask their views on the upcoming final; how they thought Tipperary might fare against arch rivals Kilkenny. The hunt for match tickets was another question which would be high on the agenda. We would spend about an hour in the square which, we thought, would give us more than enough material and hopefully meet one or two characters along the way. Then we would relocate to nearby Semple Stadium where the Tipperary team were having their final training session.

There was a member of the cornerboy fraternity on duty in Liberty Square, leaning up against the wall of the local bank. He watched with intent as Michael Lyster interviewed members of the public. It was fun, and it captured the excitement leading up to an All-Ireland Final in the town where the GAA was founded, just a few yards away in the famed Hayes' Hotel. We finished filming after about an hour and the crew packed away the sound and camera gear in the van. Next stop Semple Stadium! That's when our cornerboy sprung to life and approached Michael Lyster.

'Ye never asked me nothin',' he complained, very annoyed.

Michael couldn't believe his ears. He pointed out to him that we had been there for over an hour and that he'd watched our every move but hadn't bothered to come near us. Now that we were finished and the gear all stacked away, he had decided to come over to complain that his views had not been sought.

'I'm 38 years folly-in' Tipperary hurlin' and ye never asked me nothin',' he stressed, as if to emphasise the gravity of our omission.

We held a quick conference on the footpath, and it was agreed that as a public relations gesture we would do one last interview with our Tipp man who felt overlooked. There was nothing for it but to wearily unpack all the heavy gear – cables, cameras etc. While the gear was being unloaded Michael explained to our man how he would do the interview. He would start by asking him how long he had been a follower of Tipperary hurling and then go on to talk about the match.

Gear set up, camera rolling, sound running, Michael speaks directly into camera.

'We are still here in the square in Thurles and I'm joined by a man who has been following hurling in Tipperary for quite a few years. How many years, exactly?'

'I'm 38 years folly-in' hurlin' in Tipperary,' he replied proudly, obviously delighted with himself.

'So tell me,' said Michael, 'What do you think of their prospects on Sunday?'

'They haven't a fuckin' hope in hell!'

And he was gone! He marched up the square, no doubt delighted with himself, and to his credit, he never once looked back to see our reaction. He had struck a blow of defiance and had showed Michael Lyster and his crowd from RTÉ just what he thought of them. It was brilliant, and we fell around the street laughing. The 'interview' never saw the light of day.

Ossie Bennett – The Masseur

Just a few miles outside Thurles on the main Dublin to Cork N8 lies the small town of Johnstown. In the early 1970s, I went to a match in Thurles with the late Mick Dunne, his lovely wife Lily and his daughter Eileen, the RTÉ newsreader. Mick was doing the match commentary that day. My father was an avid fan of Mick Dunne's match reports in *The Irish Press* before he left the paper to join RTÉ. It was the gospel according to Mick, as far as my father was concerned. As we left Thurles after the match, Mick mentioned to me that he had to call into a friend of his in Johnstown on the way back to Dublin. That was the first time I met Osmond (Ossie) Bennett. We remained friends until his sad passing in 2009.

Ossie Bennett was born in West Cork in 1916. He led a most incredible life and made an immense contribution to Irish society. He could talk for Ireland and he captivated me that first evening with his tales, as we ate a wonderful meal served up by Betty, Ossie's charming wife.

Life was turbulent in Ireland when Ossie was growing up. The fallout from the Civil War bothered him greatly, and he often told me how sad it made him to see members of the same family turn on one another during that tragic period in our past.

In 1939, just at the start of the Second World War, Ossie's uncle told him that he 'was stuck for a fireman'. Ossie joined the Irish merchant navy as a second engineer at the most dangerous time in the history of the navy. Ireland had declared its neutrality at the outbreak of the conflict, but for those serving on Irish merchant ships during the war years, there were no guarantees that our neutrality would be respected.

Ossie first served on *The Kerrymore*, sailing to and from England, bringing much-needed goods to a very isolated Ireland. He went on to serve on *The Irish Poplar*, bringing eight tons of sugar from the West Indies, and on *The Irish Fir*. He told me about a frightening incident which occurred while sailing off the coast of Newfoundland, on board *The Irish Fir*. A German U-boat fired a torpedo at the ship, and as the vessel rose up on the swell, the torpedo passed harmlessly underneath. The U-boat did not fire a second torpedo because as she rose on the swell, the tricolour, which was painted on the sides of all Irish merchant navy ships during the war, was clearly visible to the captain of the German submarine. The painted tricolour had served its purpose.

Ossie married Betty in 1949 and that was the end of his days at sea. In his living room in Johnstown, there's a beautiful model of an Irish merchant ship, complete with the painted tricolour.

Nowadays, we take for granted the back-up facilities associated with teams, be they football, hurling, soccer or rugby. We are all familiar with the physio, the masseur, the specialist trainer, the backs' coach, the forwards' coach. They are an accepted part of sport in today's world. Ossie Bennett was a pioneer in the field of sports massage in the days when it was virtually unknown. He told me once that he used 'to do the rubbing for the local athletes', and that was how he became the masseur for his first-ever team, Coolderry hurling club in Offaly. From there, he went to Toomevara, and in 1960 he was the masseur for the winning

Tipperary team in that year's All-Ireland Final.

By the time he reached the end of his career, he had been the masseur for 12 winning All-Ireland teams from 4 different counties – Tipperary, Cork, Offaly and Galway. Ossie's son, William, followed in his father's footsteps and also took to 'doing the rubbing'. In the two All-Ireland hurling finals of 1981 and 1985, father and son were on opposing sides, with Ossie being on the winning team on both occasions. William eventually finished up on the winning side with Tipperary in the two finals of 1989 and 1991. In 1995, William's talents were given the recognition they deserved when he was appointed as the masseur to the Irish rugby team, a position he still held in 2009.

Ossie – the Vintage Car Enthusiast

Ossie has another passion in life when he's not involved with hurling and football teams. That passion is engines and vintage cars. Motorists on the Cork road regularly pull up at the Bennett garage to admire the beautiful steamroller when it's parked in the forecourt. He has brought that famous steamroller to festivals and rallies the length and breadth of Ireland. There's a beautiful companion which accompanies the steamroller. It's a miniature model of the larger machine, exact in every detail and in perfect working order.

But Ossie's pride and joy is carefully stowed away in the garage, covered in tarpaulin. That's his 1901 *De Dion Bouton* vintage car, registration number MI–1. The car is in pristine condition, but what makes it unique is the fact that it is the first-ever registered car in Europe. A number of times each year, the *De Dion* is taken out of the mothballs and brought to various events around the midlands. But it comes into its own each November when Ossie takes it to one of the most famous vintage car rallies in the world – the London to Brighton rally.

For over 20 years, Ossie had been trying to persuade me to go with him on this rally, and I had managed, during all that time, to find a reason not to go. It was not my cup of tea. That was until 1989. I was on my way home from a match in Cork and, as usual, called in to him in Johnstown for a chat. Ossie was talking for Ireland, as ever, and he broached the subject once again. I was in a hurry to get on the road and agreed that yes, I would go with him the following November. Three days later, a letter arrived confirming that I would be his passenger and with details of hotel reservations in London and Brighton, which had already been made. That was it. There was no backing out now. I was going to be a less-than-enthusiastic passenger, embarking on a 55-mile drive, in a 98-year-old car, being driven by a man who was then 83 years of age. As I flew to London on that Saturday morning in November, I wondered what I had let myself in for.

Ossie greeted me on my arrival at our hotel in Kensington. He and Pat Delaney, a mechanic who works in Ossie's garage in Johnstown, had loaded the *De Dion* on to a trailer the previous day, driven to Rosslare, and taken the ferry to Fishguard. They drove to London, unloaded their precious cargo and parked both cars in the underground car park at the hotel. Pat gave the *De Dion* a special polish on the Saturday afternoon in order to have it looking its best at the starting line in Hyde Park the next morning.

Slowly it began to dawn on me that this was serious business. I was glad that I had brought the camcorder along. My son, Dara, was studying at North London University at the time, and he joined us in the hotel where we watched the final of the Rugby World Cup in the afternoon. After the match, Ossie told us to be ready to leave at 7 p.m. to go for dinner, where he would give me the timetable for the following day. Dinner was at the opulent Royal Automobile Club in Pall Mall. As he looked around at the splendour of the surroundings, Ossie said to me, with a wicked glint in his eye, 'Christ, haven't we Irishmen come a long way!'

Dinner was superb, and the conversation even better. We talked about Irish history at length, and Ossie regretted that he had never visited the museum in Kilmainham. He was curious about the artefacts that were housed in the museum, and I gave him a long list of what he could expect to see if he ever visited. One of the items on display, I told him, was the side-arm that Michael Collins was wearing when he was shot at Béal na Bláth.

'They may think they have Collins' side-arm, but they don't,' he stated firmly, 'And don't ask me any more about it because I'm saying nothing.'

He refused to elaborate any further, despite my best efforts to probe him. Instead he went on to give me the rundown on what would happen the next day. He had arranged a 5 a.m. call for himself, Pat and myself. The hotel would be serving breakfast at 5.30 a.m., as there were several other guests who were going on the 'run'. (Those on the inside track don't refer to the rally as a journey to Brighton, it's simply the 'run'.)

Ossie and I would leave the hotel at 6.15 a.m., aboard the *De Dion* and drive to the starting point at Hyde Park. Pat would take the car and trailer to Brighton and meet up with us later. He had it all worked out with military precision, but of course, he'd been doing this run for over 30 years.

Now with dinner almost over, he wanted us to finish up and go back to the hotel, with more than a hint that he did not want Pat and I to stay up late. The 5 a.m. alarm call had already made up my mind for me. My only worry now was would the RTÉ cameraman turn up on time in the morning.

About two weeks earlier, I went to Ed Mulhall in the RTÉ newsroom to tell him that Ossie was about to do his thirty-third London-Brighton run, and that I felt the story was newsworthy. Ed knows a good news story and agreed. He suggested that I talk to Brian O'Connell, the

RTÉ London editor, to set the train in motion. Brian arranged that the RTÉ cameraman in London would meet up with us in the hotel at 5.30 a.m.

I need not have worried. At 5.30 a.m. on the dot, Tony joined us for breakfast, and by 6.15 a.m. Ossie, Tony and I were chugg-chugging along the road up to Hyde Park on a still dark Sunday morning in a 1901 car that had to take Ossie and I 55 miles to the south coast of England.

The scale of this London to Brighton rally fully dawned on me when we reached the starting point. There were huge crowds gathered along the roads leading out of Hyde Park. Everywhere there were marshals in yellow hazard-bibs directing cars to their correct starting places. The slower cars would leave first, and we were certainly in that category. Tony and I needed to get the news story out of the way as quickly as possible. I explained to Ossie that I would ask him to describe the car to us, what it meant to him to take part each year and why he kept coming back year after year. He played a 'blinder', showing the camera round the car. Four passenger seats, two of them facing the driver, no roof and a long steel handle for steering, similar to a tiller on a boat. He told us about his excitement before heading off and then he blew it.

'And I want to say how delighted I am that my old pal, Tadhg de Brún from RTÉ, is with me on the run this year,' enthused Ossie.

Cut!

We explained to him that he could not mention me at all and that this business was entirely about him. I finished off the package by asking him why he keeps coming back.

'I'll do it for as long as I can – we'll all be a long time dead.'

Ossie – The London–Brighton Drive

And then, at a few minutes after seven, we were on our way, just as the sun was appearing over the London horizon. Tony sat in front, looking backwards, filming Ossie's face which was etched in concentration as we headed into the London traffic. There are no special policing arrangements for cars participating in the rally, and 520 of them were heading for Brighton that morning. You join the traffic just as you would in your saloon car on your way to work.

It was exhilarating. Crowds lined the pavements as we made our way under Big Ben and past the House of Commons. We dropped Tony off after a few miles, and he went back to the RTÉ studio to send back his footage, by satellite link, to the newsroom in Donnybrook.

'Tadhg boy, we're flying!' Ossie remarked, as we made our first pit-stop outside Crawley. The car needed an oil refill at regular intervals and this would be the first of two, all going well. The road south was a long line of vintage cars being driven by people from all walks of life and from several different countries. At one point we passed what looked like an umbrella on wheels, and I was glad that I had brought a second 90-minute cassette for the camcorder. We went through a checkpoint in Croyden, where there were vast crowds. The checkpoint would prove that we had, in fact, driven all the way and not hitched a lift on the back of a trailer.

By 9.30 a.m. we were well on our way and had left London far behind us. It was a beautiful, crisp morning and Ossie assured me we were making good time, and that we would make our second stop shortly. We left the A23 just south of Horley and pulled into a layby just beside Gatwick airport. There waiting for us was Pat, Ossie's sister Mary, and her husband Peter Normandale. Peter and Mary lived in Dorset, where Peter was a general practitioner, and every year on the day of the Brighton run, they would drive to this meeting point. We were more than ready for a second breakfast, and Mary did not disappoint us. She had a car-boot full of goodies for us, steaming hot tea and coffee and a large bottle of brandy to warm us up on a cold winter's morning.

It was a pit-stop in the real sense. Pat tended to the car while the rest of us gorged ourselves on the goodies Mary had brought up from Dorset. We were joined by two men who were selling poppies on the side of the road. They did not make a sale to us that morning, but Ossie poured them two cups of brandy and they drank to our health and wished us a safe journey. We were ready for what we hoped would be the last leg of the run. Mary and Peter would drive back to Brighton and meet us at the finishing line. Pat would come with Ossie and I, as this part of the route would put the car to the test.

There were two steep climbs on the A273, Burgess Hill and Pyecombe Hill. Large crowds lined this part of the route, waving Union Jacks and shouting encouragement to each car as it struggled up the hills at walking pace. There were lines of Landrovers parked all along the road. Ossie told me they were there for the cars that might not make the climb and would have to be towed to Brighton. We rejoined the A23 and a roadside signpost told us it was just five miles to Brighton.

The crowds on the pavement grew as we neared the finishing line. I was taken aback at the number of people who had turned out all along the way, but as we turned down at The Sealife Centre onto Madeira Drive, it was like being at a football match. We crossed the finish line just after 12.30 p.m., the twenty-third car home up to that point. Ossie was cheering, Pat was waving to the crowd and I was elated, but I still had the camera rolling. This was too good to miss. It had been an amazing experience, and I would have been quite happy to go back to London and start all over again. As we crossed the line, the public address announcer approached the car to interview Ossie.

'All the way from Ireland, Osmond Bennett. Congratulations! Did you have a good run from London?'

Ossie replied that we had a trouble-free run all the way.

'What a wonderful man you are, Osmond. How many times have you completed the run?'

Ossie told him that this was his thirty-third time to finish the run.

'Ladies and gentlemen, what an achievement at the ripe old age of 83. Thank you Osmond Bennett.'

Then it was time to get the car to the hotel and load it onto the trailer for the journey back to Ireland the next day. We were staying in The Grand Hotel, which had been in the news a few years earlier for all the wrong reasons – the bombing of the Tory Party conference. It had been fully refurbished and restored to its former glory and is indeed a wonderful hotel.

When we had all checked into the hotel, Ossie told us it was time to go to bed. This was not a statement, it was an order. He wanted us all to be well rested for the Veteran Car Club Of Great Britain banquet which was being held in the hotel that night. Róisín Duffy of RTÉ called me from the newsroom in Donnybrook to tell me that she had the footage from London and that it all looked great. She had put a 'voiceover' on it, and it would be on the Six o'clock and Nine o'clock news that evening, including the interview with Ossie. The banquet was a splendid affair, and Ossie's exploits were given special mention at it.

When dinner was over that night, I suggested to him that he might call home. He was gone a long time, but I'll never forget his comment when he came back.

'Tadhg boy, the phone at home is melting there are so many people calling to say they saw me on the News!'

I was thrilled for him. It was great that this amazing man got the recognition for his wonderful achievement.

His 90th birthday party was held in the Kilkenny Court Hotel, and he drove to the hotel in the *De Dion*. His family had tried to arrange a 'surprise' party for him, but he phoned me himself to invite me to it! Ossie Bennett passed away in 2009. He'll be sorely missed by all who knew him. The *De Dion* was parked at his graveside, and it was a poignant reminder of a wonderful weekend I had spent with him.

Harmless Rivalry

I stood in the tunnel in Croke Park on a hurling final day many years ago with John Motson, the legendary BBC soccer commentator. He was captivated by the atmosphere, but was quite taken aback too.

'Goodness me! The fans are not segregated. Will there be trouble?'

I assured him that there would be no trouble, that the fans would leave the ground together after the match and head for their favourite pubs to celebrate or drown their sorrows. Motson was amazed. He said that he wished it could be the same at football matches all over England.

We are fortunate to have it this way, and hopefully it will remain so. That is not to say that there are no great rivalries between teams in Ireland! In rugby there's no greater rivalry than the one between Leinster and Munster. At club level, you have Shannon and Garryowen in Limerick. The inter-county rivalry in the GAA is fierce but friendly, especially along county boundaries. It's different from the rivalry we have seen at times at cross-channel soccer matches, which is naked tribalism or even outright hatred.

A few years ago I saw a wonderful example of inter-county rivalry. Cork fans who came to Dublin by road for the 2007 hurling final would have seen a huge roadside banner as they passed through Kilkenny which read, '*From Ó'hAilpín to Has-been in 70 minutes!*'

Just in case anyone missed it on the way up, the banner had been moved to the other side of the road for their journey home.

Strange banners and signs along the road always seem to catch my attention. I once saw a hand-painted sign outside Omagh which read, 'Freshly dug potatoes from Dublin' – a slight contradiction. My favourite was one I saw in Kerry. When the Council completed the new stretch of road outside Castleisland a few years ago, they decided to erect a sign which would remind road-users how promptly they had gone about their work. The sign read, 'Castleisland by-pass. Completed three months ahead of schedule.' The local artist was obviously pleased with this, and he painted a new sign underneath. 'Fair play to ye lads!'

I earnestly hope that the sporting rivalry which exists here in Ireland retains the good humour and banter which makes it special. We are fortunate that large crowds of people can flock to venues like Thomond Park, Thurles or Castlebar to enjoy a good game without even a hint of crowd trouble.

Mention of Castlebar reminds me of a Connacht final a few years ago. It was a fresh, sunny day but the weather forecasters warned that there might be rain in the afternoon. There were two gentlemen sitting in the front garden of a house across from McHale Park. I asked them if they thought it would stay dry. The answer to my question left me just as wise as before I asked it.

'There might be the odd shower, but it won't rain!'

The 'Live' Draw

If there's one thing that can send shivers of fear down the spine on *The Sunday Game*, it's the draw for the next round of qualifiers, or the 'back-door' draw if you prefer. These draws are fraught with danger as there are so many elements which can go wrong. In recent years, we have conducted the draw at a match venue after the live game. Two sets of balls are used, one set for the rehearsal draw and another for the live transmission. Normally, the draw is conducted indoors, but a few years ago we conducted the draw in the main stand in Fitzgerald Stadium in Killarney.

Not surprisingly, a large crowd gathered to watch, which was not a problem. I borrowed a megaphone from a Garda in the stand and explained to the crowd that we were about to do a rehearsal draw, stressing that this was not the real thing. We would be going live in about 20 minutes, I told them.

Marty Morrissey and Seán Kelly, President of the GAA, then conducted the rehearsal draw flawlessly. We then filled the two drums with the balls for the live draw, and it too went without a hitch. It was time to head for Dublin. We walked back to our cars, carrying with us the two draw drums and the set of balls. Marty was in for a bit of stick from a member of the public.

'Marty Morrissey – that was a shite draw you gave us.'

Marty asked him how he could have known about the draw when he was not watching the television.

'I wasn't watchin' the telly, but me brother was up in the stand and he phoned me mobile to tell me the draw. And it's a shite draw.'

We discussed some of the other pairings thrown up by the draw, and it soon became apparent that something was amiss. It transpired that his brother had phoned him after the rehearsal draw (so much for my warning) so he really did not know which teams had been paired together. We gave him the right pairings and he seemed much happier with his county's prospects, so much so that he even offered to help us carry the drums back to our cars.

A Tale of Two Salmon

There were sideline seats in front of the Hogan Stand in Croke Park and access to these seats was through the tunnel only, which created some problems for the poor cameraman trying desperately to keep his camera steady and his view clear as crowds made their way to and from the seats. Despite all this, the cameraman in the tunnel was actually one of the most popular people in the ground because his camera showed the vast majority of the crowd shots on match days. People would make their way down the steps from their seats and ask to be shown on the television, no doubt to let their neighbours know that they were in the best seats on All-Ireland day. One of the regular visitors down to us was Martin Thornton, the well-known boxer from Spiddal in County Galway. He would greet me the same way each time.

'*Scáil a' lampa orm!*' (Shine the lamp on me.)

Martin would stand next to the tunnel until we assured him that we had, indeed, 'shined the lamp' on him, and that Mícheál O'Hehir, who knew him well, had referred to the fact that he was at the match. On the day of an All-Ireland semi-final in the early 1970s, we 'shone the lamp' on Martin and he promised our cameraman, the late Bill Robinson, and myself that he would see us for the final. He was as good as his word, and he arrived down the steps of the stand on the day of the final with two large rolls of newspaper, which he presented to Bill and myself. This was his way of thanking us for 'shining the lamp' on him. Inside the two rolled-up newspapers were two beautiful fresh salmon, weighing at least seven pounds each. He was incorrigible. A man in Galway told me a great story about Martin which is worth telling.

The tale has it that Martin filled up a bag with old Irish half-crowns which he then took to New York and sold as souvenir coins of the great Irish racehorse Arkle, at the knockdown price of $5 each. If the story was true, it would be headline news in the business world.

The Missing Tipp Trousers

At a function in Tullamore, not long after the famous 1982 football final, a member of the victorious Offaly team told me a wonderful story about a Tipperary man who went to the hurling final a few years earlier to support his native county. The man in question lived on a farm with his widowed mother, a few miles outside Thurles. He intended to travel to Dublin by train on the day before the match. His mother suggested to him that he might buy himself a new suit for his trip to the capital, and he duly went to a draper's shop in Thurles and carried out her instructions before boarding the train. The draper who sold him the suit suggested that he might put the clothes he was wearing in a bag, so that he could wear his new purchase on the train, but the Tipp man rejected his advice and told the draper to put the new suit into a bag. He had already made his own plans regarding the suit.

The railway line passed through his farm a few miles outside Thurles, and as soon as the train pulled out of the station he went into the toilet and took the suit out of the draper's bag. He then removed the 'old clothes' he was wearing, put them in the bag, and as the train passed close to the house minutes later, he threw the bag out the window. His mother would collect the bag beside the railway-line and put the clothes in the wash before his return on Monday. But he hadn't checked the clothes hanger. To his horror he discovered, too late, that there was only a jacket on that hanger. The draper had forgotten to put the trousers in the bag. He was now faced with a major problem as he stood in the toilet of the Dublin train in his Y-fronts.

The only person who could come to his aid was the ticket collector, so he stuck his head round the door of the toilet and waited until the ticket man came along. He explained his dilemma. The man from Iarnród Éireann was sympathetic, but could do nothing to solve the problem there and then. He said that he would knock on the door later and, hopefully, have a solution.

A short while later, the ticket collector returned to the toilet with good news and bad news. The bad news was that the Tipp man would have to remain in the toilet until the train reached Heuston Station in Dublin. The good news was that the ticket collector would go to the lost property office in the station and, hopefully, he could get a pair of trousers that would fit the stranded man in the toilet.

They did find a pair to fit him, and he was able to escape from his prison two hours later. But the man who told me the story was worried that he had shared it with me, and with good reason.

'Don't tell that story to anyone de Brún, cos I think it was a cousin of me mother's that it happened to, and she'd be ragin' that I told someone.'

It's a story you could not make up, and I will protect the identity of the man who told it to me. I don't know if the episode had any repercussions for the draper in Thurles.

Choppers, Boats & Near Misses

There were quite a few 'near-misses' in the early days of live TV broadcasting, but people seemed to take them in their stride, as they were part of the excitement of live television. Today, we take satellite link-up from match venues for granted, but it wasn't always like this. When RTÉ recorded games in towns around Ireland which were to be shown on *The Sunday Game* that night, the match tape had to be sent to Dublin to be edited into a highlights package. A fast car would be ready after the game, and often with the help of An Garda Síochána, the tape was dashed to Dublin.

There was a special arrangement in place in Páirc Uí Chaoimh in Cork. The Cork ground is situated on the banks of the Lee, on the opposite side of the river from the Dublin road. This meant that the fast car would have to go into Cork city, cross the river and make its way out the Dublin road. This would entail a huge delay in getting the match tape to Dublin, and a solution had to be found to speed up the process.

So on match days, a boatman was hired who would take the tape across the river where the fast car would be waiting on the opposite riverbank for delivery of its precious cargo. The system broke down however when on one particular match day, the boatman was paid for his services before the game and he decided to sample the local brew on a sunny afternoon in Cork. When the tape was brought to the banks of the Lee for transportation to Dublin, the boatman was nowhere to be found.

In later years, helicopters were hired to bring back match tapes from far-flung venues like Killarney, Cork, Galway and Castlebar. Those of us working at those venues would look with envy as the helicopter took off, knowing that those on board would be back in Donnybrook in an hour, while we would face into traffic chaos. The need for helicopters soon became redundant, as tapes could be brought to a local transmitter, which was able to send the signal to RTÉ in Donnybrook.

Later, as regional studios opened in the main towns and cities around the country, it became possible to send the match pictures from there. In the earlier years, these tapes were large, bulky and expensive. There was a 60-minute tape and a 90-minute tape. On match days two tapes were used, one for each half. When the match recording eventually made its way to RTÉ, it was not unusual for an editor to be still working on the second-half, while the first-half was on the air.

The fast car, the boatman in Cork and helicopters all became surplus to requirements once matches began to be transmitted live back to RTÉ by a microwave link, direct to editing. This created a small cottage industry for the RTÉ Sports and Social Club, which is situated on the campus in Donnybrook. It was possible to send the incoming pictures and commentary from games all over the country down to the large screen in the club. For a few years the club did a roaring trade on many a Sunday afternoon, as it was now in a position to advertise that it would have 'live' coverage of a particular match on a particular date. Club members were in a position to invite friends in to watch the Munster or Connacht finals 'live', and it was regarded as a great perk, which of course it was.

The fact that these games were being shown in the RTÉ club added a further burden to anyone near a microphone at the match venue, especially the commentator. It wasn't just the match coverage which was available in the club, but also the normal chatter which goes on prior to the game, at half-time and after the game when interviews are being conducted on the sideline with players or managers. Off-the-record comments are likely to be made and are certainly not for public consumption.

10
Battles in Ballsbridge

Ulster First – in Lansdowne

In recent years, Munster and Leinster have been the dominant Irish forces in the European Heineken Cup. Two famous Munster victories were followed by Leinster's triumph in 2009. But it should be remembered that it was Ulster who led the way on an amazing day in Lansdowne Road. It was 31 January, 1999.

The campaign got off to a shaky start: a home draw with Edinburgh and a 38–3 defeat away to Toulouse, the aristocrats of European rugby. However, things soon improved due to two good wins against Ebbw Vale and Edinburgh. Harry Williams, who managed Ulster, had achieved his first objective, which was to get out of the pool stage and reach a quarter-final. More important still, that quarter-final would be a home game at Ravenhill. Hot favourites Toulouse came to Belfast and were sent packing on a night of high drama and pouring rain. Ulster were in the semi-final. Now they needed Lady Luck to smile on them again, and she did.

Another home draw, but a difficult one against another top-class French side, Stade Francais. Ulster once again were given the role of underdogs, a role which they refused to accept. In a blistering game they beat the French side 33–27 and found themselves looking forward to a European final. Better still, the venue for the final was pre-ordained before the tournament got under way. It was Lansdowne Road. The hunt started for tickets.

Less than a year before that final, an historic milestone was reached in Belfast with the signing of the Good Friday Agreement. George

Mitchell (who had been sent to Ulster by US President Clinton), Tony
Blair, Mo Mowlam and Bertie Ahern presided over long and tough
negotiations with no guarantee of a successful outcome. Ahern's mother
died during the negotiations, and he returned to Dublin for her funeral
but was back in Belfast a few hours after her burial. With the tantalising
possibility of a peaceful end to the Troubles, delays could not be
afforded. Euphoria, not just in Ireland, but worldwide, greeted the
announcement that agreement had been reached between the parties.
There was a sense that after 30 years of bloody conflict, this was a new
beginning, that there was no going back. The Irish people, north and
south, were asked to vote on the agreement. They gave their approval
overwhelmingly.

It was against this backdrop that Ulster came to Lansdowne Road
to play Colomiers, another strong French side, in the European Cup
Final. But this final was different. Irrespective of class, creed or political
persuasion, all of Ulster, and indeed all of Ireland, had got behind this
team. There was an enormous outpouring of goodwill. In the few days
before the game, messages from all over Ireland poured into the team
hotel. President McAleese and Prime Minister Tony Blair sent personal
greetings to the team and wished them well. But what surprised most
was the huge number of cards and faxes which came from GAA clubs
and counties from around the country, particularly from Ulster. Team
manager Harry Williams saw the potential this had. He arranged to have
the hundreds of messages posted on a wall in the team hotel. Players
could read those messages and realise the depth of support for the team.
It was a huge morale booster.

Lansdowne Road on match day was a sea of red and white. I was
fascinated by the array of flags, jerseys and banners on display that day.
There were hundreds of flags with the red hand of Ulster emblazoned
on them with the crown above. Side by side with them were flags with
the same red hand, without the crown, but with the letters *Tír Eoghain*

or *Doire*. There were red and white Derry City shirts and a good smattering of Cork jerseys to be seen. My favourite banner read *Ulster says Yes*. On this day, at least, Ulster was united.

The stadium erupted when the team came out to warm up. It was clear that the reception had an effect on the players. It certainly affected the French side. I could see from their body language that it unnerved them. The temperature was racked up another few degrees when the Ulster team and subs did a lap of the pitch to roars of approval. To round it off, they lined up in front of the stand and saluted the crowd – and all this *before* the game! One wonders what the French team felt in their dressing room, listening to the barrage of noise from outside.

Colomiers started well enough, but Ulster gradually took control of the game, the forwards performing superbly. At half-time the crowd were happy with a 12–3 lead. The second-half was only a few minutes old when David Humphreys kicked a dropped goal. Ulster were on their way to victory.

The 50,000 crowd knew they were going to witness history when the superb Simon Mason kicked another two penalties. The pitch invasion, when it came, was spontaneous and enormous. Ulster became the first Irish side to win the European Cup. It was a truly memorable day.

Ray Houghton's Phantom 'Yellow Card'

In 1989, I learned a valuable lesson at a soccer game in Lansdowne Road. That lesson was that things don't always appear to be what they are. The game was a hugely important World Cup qualifier between Ireland and Malta. It was a 'must win' game for the Irish in their bid to make it to Italy for their first ever World Cup the following year. There were two games in quick succession. The team would face Hungary again at Lansdowne one week later. The final game in the group was an away game in Malta. Win all three games and Italia 90 would beckon.

Ireland were ahead by a goal, but the crowd was nervous. A second goal would calm the nerves, and we could then all look forward to the next match. Thankfully, the second goal eventually arrived and was greeted with hysteria in the stands, on the terraces and in the commentary box. George Hamilton was the commentator, and as the cheers echoed around the ground, George watched his monitor and described the goal again as he watched the slow-motion replays. Something caught my eye out on the field. The referee, notebook in hand, was having a conversation with Ray Houghton. This was serious. The referee opened the notebook and started to write. Ray had received a yellow card in a previous game, and a second one would rule him out of the upcoming game against Hungary. I whispered this information into George's ear, and he duly informed the nation that Ireland would be without Ray for the next game, and that he would be sorely missed.

The two-goal cushion proved to be enough, and Jack Charlton was in buoyant mood after the game as he looked forward to the visit of the Hungarians. That game was to be played on the following Sunday, and we needed a player interview which would be broadcast on *Sports Stadium* the day before the next match. As the players emerged from the dressing room, I asked Ray Houghton to do the interview, and he gladly agreed. As we waited to go 'into record', I asked Ray why he had been booked by the referee. He looked at me with incredulity.

'What do you mean – why was I booked? I wasn't booked!'

I told Ray that I was just curious why he had received a booking, as I hadn't seen the incident that merited it.

'But I told you already that I wasn't booked – and I should know. I was out there.'

The fact that Ray was so adamant had me really worried. Then he turned his attention to George.

'Did you say in your commentary that I was booked out there?'

George told Ray that he did say so and reminded him of the incident just after Ireland's second goal. His explanation sent shivers through me.

'The poor ref had a problem. He couldn't see who scored the goal so he asked me if I knew who got it. So I told him, and he said thanks a lot, and I said you're welcome. That was it.'

I will never forget that awful feeling of horror as I realised the magnitude of my error. To Ray's credit, he laughed it off and reminded us that he would, after all, be playing the following week. He did the interview and there was no mention of the card incident. But he did remind us about it many times in the months that followed, and I had to endure some friendly jibes for a while. It was a lesson learned the hard way.

I learned another lesson in Lansdowne on another match day. Jason McAteer is a well-known practical joker. I had known that fact from the time he first joined the Irish squad, but I had not planned on being at the wrong end of one of his pranks. We were having a chat in the dressing-room corridor as the other members of the team made their way out to the field to warm up for the game. The last player to leave the dressing room was Phil Babb. As Babb made his way up the corridor McAteer ducked inside the dressing-room door. Before he did so, at the top of his voice he shouted up the corridor:

'Hey! Black arse!'

Babb swung around instantly, and now I'm the only other person in view on the corridor with him. I was mortified. McAteer was thoroughly enjoying my embarrassment from inside the door of the dressing room. Babb put me out of my misery.

'I know that wasn't you mate, and I'm pretty sure I know who it was.'

He made his way out to the pitch and Jason re-emerged, delighted with my discomfort. He was a true character and great fun as long as you avoided being on the wrong end of his pranks. His brilliant goal against

Holland in a crucial World Cup qualifier will always be a lasting memory from Lansdowne Road.

Locking In President Robinson

Big match days anywhere share one thing in common for players, and that's pre-match nerves. Individuals deal with this in different ways, and I'm always intrigued by players' demeanour prior to a big game. Some chat away freely and don't appear to show any sign of tension, while others simply give a nod of the head and go directly to the sanctuary of the dressing room. When you notice that stadium officials are in a nervous state before a game, then one starts to worry. This was the case on a very big day in Lansdowne prior to a Five Nations international. It was the day that President Mary Robinson made her first visit there in her capacity as president. Underneath the stand, the place was buzzing with excitement as officials fretted over the timetable of the day. They stressed the importance of everything going according to schedule on the day.

The newly-elected president would be met by officials on her arrival and would then be brought to the VIP area for a cup of tea before the game. At the appointed time she would be brought out to the holding area. When both teams were lined up, the president would climb the steps leading out to the pitch, where she would be introduced to the teams by the respective captains. This was the standard protocol of the day. All the IRFU officials, who were seasoned campaigners, were well used to it. I told them that this day was no different from any other, and that it would all be fine.

But they were still nervous.

On her arrival, President Robinson, her husband Nick and the presidential party were brought to the inner sanctum. The teams and match officials took to the field and all was in readiness for the introduction of the president. There's a large iron sliding door at the bottom of the steps which lead out to the pitch, and this was manned by an official on the day. By now, the president, her army Aide and Ban Gardaí were standing in the holding area waiting to be ushered out through the iron door, which was firmly shut. On the field, the two teams were already lined up and the band was in place, ready to play the presidential salute.

'Do you think they have forgotten me?' the president asked me as I rushed to the door. The officials outside now realised that something had gone wrong, and one of them started to kick the steel door with a considerable amount of force. The noise inside was deafening, and the man inside swung open the door in rage.

'Would you stop that please. What's the matter with you?'

The man outside roared in at the door-minder.

'Would you leave the door open, the fuckin' President has to come out!'

There was no reaction from any member of the presidential party. Twenty seconds later, the President was taking the salute on the field.

Politics Come to Lansdowne

There are so many lasting memories from Lansdowne Road down the years, it is difficult to single out the better ones. The Welsh rugby team came to Dublin in 1970 in their usual cocky and brash way, clearly expecting to win. They left on the wrong end of a 14-point hammering from an Irish side that tore into them from the very first minute. The Welsh half-back partnership that day were legends in their time, Barry John and Gareth Edwards. At full back JPR Williams was a colossus in that side. That was a wonderful day to be in the old ground, to see Alan Duggan dive over the line for one of Ireland's tries. The other try-scorer that day was Ken Goodall who, without doubt, was one of the finest players in the world at the time. Goodall quit the game shortly afterwards and went to England to play rugby league.

Lansdowne hosted another international in that same year, a game which attracted a lot of attention, but for all the wrong reasons. This was the visit of the Springboks from South Africa to Dublin in January 1970. The anti-apartheid movement, the trade unions and many senior politicians were strongly opposed to the visit of the South Africans. A huge demonstration was planned for match day. The terraces were empty in Lansdowne as only 30,000 people turned up for the game. There was genuine concern for security, following the publication of a letter in *The Belfast Telegraph* prior to the game. This letter had come from the Derry Ulster Volunteer Force, and it stated that an armed unit would be sent to Dublin on match day. This unit, the letter stated, would 'take care of the Papists who would attempt to make a British game of sport impossible'.

Not to be outdone, the IRA issued a statement saying that they would take action if any demonstrators were injured on the day of the game. This 'action' would be taken against the president and committee members of the IRFU. Despite the large demonstration outside the ground, the game went ahead. A late penalty by Tom Kiernan earned Ireland a draw. Fergus Slattery, another Irish legend, made his first appearance in a green jersey that day.

Two years later, Lansdowne Road was, reluctantly, drawn into politics again. The Scottish and Welsh teams refused to travel to Dublin for their Five Nations games against the Irish. The conflict in Northern Ireland was growing increasingly bloody, and the two Unions, Scottish and Welsh, expressed their concerns for the safety of their players. This decision was deeply resented by the Irish team. England and France had already been beaten that year in London and in Paris. The possibility of a Grand Slam was very real. The non-appearance of the Scots and the Welsh put paid to that ambition.

The following year, 1973, England were due to arrive in Dublin on 10 February. The violence in Ulster was raging onwards. Speculation was rife that the English would withdraw from the fixture. But they didn't and I will never forget the moment when that England team came out onto the field for that game. Lansdowne erupted and gave them a standing ovation, which lasted at least three minutes. It was a wonderful gesture. English captain John Pullin and his team seemed a bit bewildered by it all. Ireland won the game, 18–9, but what was more important was that the match took place at all. That night at the traditional post-match dinner, Pullin drew raptures of applause again when he addressed the guests.

'We may not be very good, but at least we turn up!'

Wales had the rugby team to beat all teams in the 1970s. While I looked forward to their arrival in Lansdowne, there was usually an air of pessimism and an acceptance that the Welsh would probably win. Those Welsh teams had all the stars – Barry John, Gareth Edwards, Phil Bennet, JPR Williams and the mercurial Gerald Davies. Many a good Ireland side gave it their all in those games but the Welsh had the class, and the Triple Crown famine continued for Ireland. It was tough on one of the greatest players I've ever been privileged to see play – Willie John McBride. He was destined to be part of a side that failed to win a Triple Crown. The long wait finally ended in 1982. By 1985, Ireland had won two Triple Crowns in three years. No one would have believed at the end of the 1985 season, that it would be 19 years before an Irish team would win it again.

Well they did – in 2004. And eventually after a 61-year-wait, Ireland, captained by Brian O'Driscoll, won the Grand Slam in 2009. Sixty-one years after that 1948 Grand Slam, Jackie Kyle and his colleagues could pass on the mantle.

The 'Lost' Australian Anthem

In 1990, Jack Charlton led the Irish soccer team to a first ever appearance at a World Cup. The country ground to a halt on match days, and the team surpassed all expectations by reaching the quarter-final stages of that tournament, eventually losing out 1–0 to Italy. One year later the Irish rugby team reached the quarter-final of the rugby World Cup. Australia were the opponents that day, but the Irish would face them on their own home patch, Lansdowne.

There was huge expectation and the rugby boys were determined to go one better than Charlton's side and reach the semi-finals. In the build-up to the game, the Irish captain, Philip Matthews, said that his team could do for Irish rugby what Charlton's team had done for soccer a year earlier. Matthews went further when he said that he expected the Irish to win.

The Australians were none too happy with the comments coming from the Irish camp, but they had good reason to be unhappy when they lined up beside the Irish on match day, 20 October, 1991. For some extraordinary reason, the band didn't play the Australian national anthem, 'Advance Australia Fair', before the game. The Aussies seemed bemused, as they waited to hear their anthem, but they waited in vain.

The game started at a furious pace. Both sides showed that they were really up for this game, and from an Irish perspective, Philip Matthews led by example. It was no place for the faint-hearted, and if the Aussies were annoyed by the failure of the band to play their anthem, it seemed they were going to show it by doing all they could to win the match.

Lansdowne Road fell silent when David Campese, a brilliant Australian athlete with searing pace, crossed the line for a trade-mark try. He would score another one in the second-half, and things were starting to look ominous for the Irish. But Ralph Keyes was having a great day in a green shirt, and his place-kicking kept the Irish in touch.

Then Gordon Hamilton took off on his most famous run in an Irish jersey, and with Australians converging on him, just managed to touch the ball down. A Try! Lansdowne Road erupted. Ireland were three minutes away from a World Cup semi-final when Michael Lynagh put the Australians back in front. It was heartbreaking, but it was one of those very special Lansdowne Road days which I will never forget.

When the new Lansdowne is completed, Dublin will have two state-of-the-art stadia to equal the best in the world. The new Dublin 4 venue will officially be known as The Aviva, but to me it will always be Lansdowne.

11
Odds 'n' Ends

I have been asked many times to single out the most memorable sporting occasion of my career as floor manager with RTÉ. This is an impossible question to answer – the list of candidates has become so long after 42 years' involvement in so many different sports.

The famous Munster victory over the All Blacks in 1978 has entered the history books in the same manner as the 1916 Rising: the number of people who claim to have attended both never ceases to amaze me. I was fortunate enough to be in Thomond Park on that famous day in 31 October 1978 and it was truly unforgettable.

But how does it compare with Ireland's wonderful victory over Italy in the Giants Stadium, New Jersey, in front of fanatical supporters who outnumbered the Italians nine to one during World Cup 94? Or with the Irish victory over Holland, which ended the Dutch hopes of qualification for the 2002 World Cup and sent the Irish on their way?

The official attendance for the Ireland-England Six Nations game in Croke Park was just over 82,000 although thousands more claim to have been there on that amazing day. The emotion displayed during the playing of both national anthems was palpable. Who can forget John Hayes' tears as the crowd bellowed out the anthem? One small incident went generally unnoticed that day. At the end of the English anthem, Martin Corry stepped forward from the English line-up and applauded the crowd for their total respect. The icing on the cake of course was to follow when Ireland duly beat them out the gate.

GAA

In 1982 Offaly shattered Kerry's dream of five-in-a-row All-Ireland victories and a place in the history books. The last gasp Seamus Darby goal and the disputed push in the back that preceded it are still hotly debated almost 30 years later. That day will always stand out in my memory. The great Jack O'Shea told me many years later that the ball brushed his fingertips on the way to the net that day. Such is the margin between victory and defeat. Twelve years later, in 1994, the Offaly hurlers repeated the Houdini act in the hurling final. With time running out, Limerick were poised to win their first final since 1973. Offaly went on a scoring blitz in those last few minutes, and the game was over before the Limerick men knew what hit them. It was the stuff of dreams – or nightmares depending on your point of view. It was also a day of mixed emotions for Offaly manager Eamon Cregan, who had been a member of that victorious Limerick team 21 years earlier.

One year later brought another day of high drama in Croke Park, with the arrival of Ger Loughnane and a Clare team determined to make the breakthrough after 81 years in the wilderness. For years, Clare teams were supposedly under a curse from the famous Biddy Early, a legendary sorcerer in the county. The most common version of the story, and there are many, was that the men of the county spent too much time playing hurling, away from their wives and drinking alcohol. Biddy decided that the Claremen would never win a trophy. The curse was banished on that famous day in 1995, and there was no shortage of alcohol in the hotel that night. Before the game, Ger Loughnane promised us that he would give us a quick comment on his way back to the pitch for the second half, and he was as good as his word. His last words to Marty Morrissey on the top step of the Cusack Stand tunnel were, 'We are going to win this match'.

It was total belief in his team's ability. Clare did reach the final again two years later, and Loughnane almost out-foxed us that day. Almost. In order to ensure that our team graphic is correct, I always check with team managers when they arrive in the ground that the team in the match programme is the team that will, in fact, start the match. It is important too, that the substitutes numbers tally with those on our graphics. It was no secret that Ger was prone to springing a belated change at the eleventh hour on match days, but he assured me that day that the match programme was correct. However, just as the teams made their way across the field to be formally introduced to the President, we noticed that Fergal Hegarty, who was due to play, was on his way to the Clare dug-out.

'He has the 'flu.'

That was the hurried information we got on the sideline, and Marty did a live update seconds later on the late team change. Ger Loughnane cut it as fine as he could that day, and Marty and I were delighted with ourselves that we had spotted it in time. It was not the last time that Ger sprang a late change on us.

Rugby

I mentioned earlier the famous Munster victory over the All Blacks in Thomond Park and its place in the history books. But there were other days in the Limerick ground that were memorable, and it was a privilege to be there. In 2003 Gloucester played Munster in a now infamous Heineken Cup game, and the pre-match statistics did not make good reading. In order to progress in the tournament, Munster had to win by a margin of 27 points. In achieving that unlikely victory, they also had to score four tries and earn a bonus point. The Gloucester team were late arriving at the ground, and I was initially told that the team manager, Nigel Melville, would not be available for a pre-match interview. I decided to double check this as I had a feeling he might remember me. In 1985, he was injured in a Five Nations game (Ireland v England) in

Lansdowne Road and I went over to him to check on the nature of his injury. He was sitting on his own underneath the stand, disappointed at having to go off. I offered him a bottle of water as I headed back outside.

After our second request for an interview, Melville agreed. I like to think that the bottle of water in 1985 played a role in getting us that interview in 2003.

Munster did the impossible that day. They got the four tries required and won by 27 points, the last two of which came from a Ronan O'Gara conversion with time running out. There were quite a few Gloucester supporters in the crowd, and they were truly shell-shocked. It was one of those sporting events that will be talked about for years to come. Chatting to us after he had completed his post-match television interview with Tracy Piggott, Nigel summed it up.

'We've just been mugged!'

A year later, Gloucester returned to Thomond Park to take on Munster again in the Heineken Cup. After the game, which Munster won, Melville once again summed it up perfectly.

'We've just been mugged again!'

Incidentally, as a supposedly impartial touchline reporter, Tracy Piggott is anything but and has to be restrained, sometimes physically, from running up and down the field following the play. Tracy truly gets involved in a match.

One final word on Thomond Park. I was back there for the AIL (All-Ireland League) final in 2009, and I needed to use a room as a make-up area for 'the talent'. Helpful as always, the Thomond staff told me I could have the doping room. When we were finished I returned the key and picked up a titbit of information along the way.

'Do you know that we call the doping room the Reggie Corrigan room now?'

This was news to me, and the man in Limerick explained how this came about. Munster played a Heineken Cup game at the ground some months earlier in 2009 and won the match comfortably, 40-plus points to 5. Reggie, I was informed, was co-commentator for Sky Sports that day, and had chosen as his 'man of the match' the French player who scored the five points for the opposition. The doping room in Thomond Park was duly renamed the Reggie Corrigan Room. Sorry Reggie!

Boxing

21 March 2009 was a red-letter day for Irish sport. The Irish rugby team faced the Welsh in Cardiff with the elusive Grand Slam and Triple Crown up for grabs. Later that night, Bernard Dunne got into the ring in the O2 Arena. Victory would make him a champion of the world. I worked at ringside that night and, like many of the great sporting occasions, it was a privilege to be there.

In 2007, Kiko Martinez floored Bernard 86 seconds into Round 1 of a fight which Bernard was expected to win. It was a major setback in his boxing career. Marty Morrissey and I were ringside that night and I got a text message from a colleague next morning which read, 'Congratulations! You and Morrissey spent more time in the ring last night than Bernard Dunne!'

Cruel. Bernard is made of strong stuff, and he fought his way back into contention again. He got the opportunity to become world champion on the night of 21 March.

The first fight of the evening was watched by only a handful of spectators in the arena. Outside, large crowds were gathered in the various bars, all of them watching the Ireland/Wales game in Cardiff. There was a huge screen inside the arena where the boxing spectators could also watch as events unfolded in Cardiff. By the time Jim Rock and Elessio Forlan squared up to one another in the ring, there was quite a good crowd in to see the fight, and the situation in Cardiff was becoming a little precarious. Wales had taken the lead, and only five minutes remained. When Ronan O'Gara's drop goal attempt sailed over the bar, the O2 Arena erupted, inside and out. Rock and Forlan paused momentarily, seemed to realise what was happening and then continued fighting. Moments later the entire complex erupted again when Stephen Jones' last gasp penalty dropped short. It was an incredible moment and set the tone for what was to come.

World champion Katie Taylor finally got an opportunity to show an Irish boxing audience just how special a talent she is with a resounding victory over American Caroline Barry, roared on by a now capacity crowd of 9,000. It was wonderful that the amateur was given the opportunity to box on such an important night of Irish professional boxing.

The build-up to the main event reached a climax when Marty Morrissey climbed into the ring and introduced the horde of VIPs to the crowd. High up in the studio overlooking the ring, Darragh Maloney and his panel discussed the main event which was almost upon us. All agreed that this would be a tough night for Bernard.

On big sporting occasions such as this, the floor manager is fortunate to be right in the thick of things. The arrival of the fighters is all co-ordinated to suit the TV schedule, and the promoters of the event are in constant liaison with the floor manager throughout the evening. Bernard had to be first into the ring, as he was the challenger. At the appointed hour, I went to his dressing room and informed his people that it was time to go. It had been decided that Bernard would enter the arena alone and would only be joined by his ringside team when he reached the end of a long sloping ramp which was surrounded by a big group of drummers. I took him to the top of the ramp and showed him his starting position, behind a white gauze curtain which was back-lit and would show him in silhouette to the now hysterical crowd. He seemed to be there for an eternity as I counted down the clock to him.

'Twenty seconds Bernard. Ten seconds Bernard. Go for it.'

He winked at me just as the curtain dropped and then slowly made his way down the ramp and into the ring.

An hour later he was champion of the world. He had come through a gruelling fight, and his opponent, Ricardo Cordoba, had proved himself to be one tough customer. As soon as the fight ended, Marty and myself climbed into the ring and set ourselves up for the interview. It was mayhem. During the course of the interview, I felt myself being kicked on the foot. On looking down to investigate, I could see that it was Cordoba's leg that was hitting me. He was still being treated on the canvas directly behind me. I did not look down a second time and was relieved when the medical people took him away on a stretcher. The morning after the fight, I noticed two blobs of congealed blood on one of my shoes. It was a grim reminder of the bruising battle Bernard had been through in order to become world champion.

A few weeks after the fight, Bernard came to RTÉ to celebrate his association with the Sports Department. He came to say thanks. During this visit, Jimmy Magee told us about an incident which had occurred a few days after the fight, when Bernard visited his former school in Neilstown. Sitting at a table having refreshments, Jimmy overheard him saying, 'Sir, would you pass the milk please?'

The world champion still calling his former teacher 'sir'! It's a measure of the man.

Bernard defended his title six months later on 26 September 2009 at the O2 Arena in Dublin. The challenger hailed from Thailand and boxed under the name Poonsawat Kratingdaenggym, a commentator's nightmare if ever there was one. His real name was Chalermwong Udomna, which was a little more manageable. His record spoke for itself: 27 wins by knock-out and only one defeat in his professional career. Before the fight, the experts said it could be a tough night for Dunne, and they were proved right. It all seemed to be going well enough but in the third round Bernard was on the floor three times. The referee had no option but to stop the fight. His world title was gone. What struck me most after the fight ended was the total silence which fell over the vast arena. People cried all around the ringside. Once again, Marty and I climbed into the ring, not knowing for sure if there was going to be an interview. Bernard did not even wait to be asked. He come over to Marty and said he was sorry for letting everyone down. The crowd cheered him to the rafters. Bernard Dunne did not need to apologise to the Irish people. He has been a wonderful champion and a great ambassador for Irish sport.

Looking at the above collection of great sporting moments, you will understand why it is impossible to single out any one as the greatest of all. I could easily have added another 100 to the list. Hopefully, these few selected memories will give a flavour of the variety, intensity, and excitement which I have experienced over the past 40 years on the job.

12
Final Wrap

Technology

In the 40-plus years that I have been involved in the broadcasting of sport, the changes that have taken place in technology have been truly staggering. From the early days in Croke Park when 3 or 4 cameras were the norm, 20-plus cameras are now almost standard on major match days. On All-Ireland final days, one of those cameras is not even in the ground itself, but high up on a crane which is parked in the grounds of nearby Clonliffe College. This camera provides a wonderful shot of the stadium and the streets surrounding it. Having once, very briefly, taken a trip up in the bucket, I can assure the reader that it is not a place you want to visit. The person operating that camera requires a very good head for heights and, just as important, a very strong bladder. In my early days as a cameraman, I heard many stories of colleagues who brought a bucket up with them to the camera tower in Punchestown or the Curragh. Those stories I'm sure were mythical but I can assure you that after a few hours in one of those towers, the first port of call when we got off the air was a toilet.

Instant 'slo-mo' replays are now the accepted norm of television match coverage. The picture output from half a dozen cameras are recorded throughout a game. Those images are available for transmission within seconds of an incident taking place. When I started out in television this was unheard of. Rugby has taken this one step further with the arrival of the TMO, the television match official. When the match day referee and his team arrive in the ground, I meet up with the TMO and bring him to our outside broadcast truck and introduce him to the match director and the video tape personnel, who will show him the replays if he has to award a try or disallow it. If the TMO is called upon to adjudicate on a try during the course of a game, he will inform Michael Fitzgerald, the RTÉ match director, what his decision is prior to telling the referee. This gives Michael the chance to look out for reactions to the decision out on the field. This new innovation has worked very successfully since its inception. The debate continues regarding whether it should be used in other sports.

I have been asked many times by players of all codes how many cameras are recording at all times during a game, and I have given them all the same answer.

'You are being recorded at all times during a game, even if the ball is 70 yards away.'

It's a long time since we stuck the letters and scores onto the blackboard in Croke Park and Woodbrook. When I look at the graphics which are available now, I never cease to be amazed at the advances that have been made. Post-match analysis has also entered into a new phase. Studio experts can now move arrows and circles around the screen to demonstrate a section of the action as it unfolded during a game. The video tape boys and the editors love this relatively new 'toy' and they take great pride in showing it off on the air. I can only look on in admiration at the fruits of their labour and I stay well away from it, as I have no idea how it works.

Travel

Travelling the length and breadth of the country for years has changed dramatically in more recent times. There are three major reasons for this change – the construction of motorways in Ireland, the arrival of the bypass and the mobile phone. It's not that long ago that a journey from Cork to Dublin could take up to five hours on match days. We'd crawl out the Glanmire road and slowly make our way through Fermoy and

Mitchelstown. Cashel was the next major bottleneck. Just when you thought you were making some progress, Portlaoise slowed you to a halt again. If that wasn't bad enough, you knew that Kildare, Newbridge and Naas still lay ahead, and there was no such thing as the M50. We knew we could turn off at Monasterevin and come in by the Curragh, but a lot of fellow travellers got to know about that short-cut pretty quickly.

The journeys back from places such as Galway, Limerick, Clones, Belfast, Castlebar and Killarney were long hauls through gridlocked towns and on inferior roads. The construction of the N7, the N4, the M1 and many other new roads has changed all that. The arrival of the bypass contributed greatly to the improved blood pressure levels of many of us travelling to and from matches all over the country. No more crawling through Nenagh and Navan, Longford or Limerick, Monaghan and Moate. And the good people of those towns and others were spared many sentiments of ill-will against them and their towns.

Then there is the 'rat-run'. This is the short-cut out of town on match days. Michael Lyster is an accomplished rally driver and well versed in reading Ordnance Survey maps. If there is a back road out of the match venue, Michael will find it. A small number of us have consigned these routes to memory or written them down for future reference. We now have a list of rat runs from a host of grounds around the country and, let me add, they are a closely-guarded secret. As I mentioned earlier, too many road-users got to know about the turn-off in Monasterevin. In more recent times, I've heard people discussing the turn-off at Birdhill for Thomond Park and the Gaelic Grounds in Limerick. Thankfully, I have discovered a new quick escape route out of Limerick, which you will understand I am not prepared to discuss here.

There are two rat runs out of Clones, the first of which I discovered during the last foot-and-mouth epidemic. Post-match traffic in Clones consists of long lines of cars, in all directions, going nowhere in a hurry. A friendly member of An Garda Síochána rescued me from the gridlock one Sunday in Clones. He guided me out to a side road and told me to continue on until I came to the foot-and-mouth patrol a few hundred yards down the road. There was another Garda on duty with the foot-in-mouth patrol, and he had got a call on his walkie-talkie from my Good Samaritan to say I was en route. The officials of the Department of Agriculture sprayed the car meticulously and I was free to go. The second Garda guided me up what can only be described as a series of lanes, with room for one car only, and suddenly I was on the Dublin road, well clear of the town. I wrote down the new escape route immediately. My colleague Ciaran McDonagh discovered a newer escape recently, and it will be put to good use some day.

There are many of these rat runs dotted around the country. The cross-country exit from Ballybofey is a particularly good one, as is the one from Cusack Park in Ennis, which can be a nightmare on match days. The escape route from Semple Stadium in Thurles, another creation of Michael Lyster, is without doubt the daddy of them all. Many years ago producer Michael O'Carroll showed me a new route to Dublin from Thurles which skirted Lisheen Mine, took us through Geataban and up to Carlow. I used it many times. The new Lyster route out of Thurles takes you down a narrow lane near the stadium, through three sets of cross-roads with a right-hand-turn at a red shed and eventually leads you to join the Cork road at Johnstown. Do not attempt to find this route from what I have described here, because you will finish up very, very lost on the Tipperary-Kilkenny border. Not all of my colleagues share my enthusiasm for the rat-runs. Floor Manager Don Irwin is a true Dub and tends to get lost once he passes the gates of the Phoenix Park or Newlands Cross. He now refuses to veer off on one of my detours and is happy to curse the traffic instead.

Telephones

In recent years, I have often wondered how we got by on the road without the mobile phone. Gone are the days when one had to stop in a town en route to a match, have the proper coinage and then find a phone box with a functioning phone inside. The mobile has become a lifeline in the most mundane situations.

'Howya! I'm just outside Athlone and I didn't bring a 'Man of the Match' trophy with me. Do you have a spare one with you?'

Problem solved by the mobile phone. The mobile also acts as a form of AA roadwatch amongst colleagues on the road. The most frequently received call on a journey to Cork or Thurles is, 'There's a huge tail-back in Abbeyleix. Take the detour.'

On the Limerick road, you substitute Mountrath for Abbeyleix. You can expect to make or receive the same call on the return journey. No doubt, the fine men and women of Laois County Council will eventually bypass these two fine towns, which will shorten our journeys considerably in the future.

Taverns

For me personally, the arrival of the bypass and the motorway had a downside. It took me away from many tried and trusted pub food establishments that I had got to know all over the country. Going to a night match in Thomond Park, Musgrave Park, the Brandywell or Terryland Park in Galway, it was always good to know a good eating place within a 20-mile radius of the venue. That would become the stop-off point for food which would fortify one for the long evening ahead. Toomevara in Tipperary and Craughwell in Galway are perfect examples of places where you are assured good food, a friendly service and a quick exit again in 40 minutes.

I witnessed a funny incident in the Tipperary Inn in that great hurling stronghold of Toomevara a few years ago. A gentleman at the bar finished his meal and handed the bar lady €10 in payment. She thanked him and went off about her business. A few minutes went by and I could see that the man was still at the counter and was expecting to get some change. The good lady went by a number of times until she eventually realised what was happening. She told the man that the €10 was, as she put it, 'spot on'. He waited until the next time she passed, and delivered the following line, 'Do you know what missus, yer just like the weather. No change.' He left, delighted with himself.

Before the opening of the bypass, Fermoy was a regular stop for food on the way to Musgrave Park or Turner's Cross. On one such stop I was enjoying the bacon and cabbage and the mandatory pint of milk when a regular customer arrived in and joined his friends at the bar. From the ensuing conversation, it was clear that the new arrival had been visiting a friend in hospital and the others were anxious to hear how the patient was getting on. The medical update was graphic and to the point.

'Jaysus lads he's in a desperate state up dere! Desperate! He's above in de bed with two sets of jump leads hangin' out of him!'

These are the kind of characters that the motorway and the bypass will cause me to miss in the small towns and villages on the roads of Ireland. The journey times have reduced dramatically in the last few years which, of course, is a huge positive. But I prefer to visit the smaller establishments around the country and meet the locals. In the near future, it will be possible for me to leave the house, drive a mile to the M50 and go to Galway, Limerick or Cork with dual carriageway or motorway all the way and no need to pass through a town or village. Of course it's huge progress in road-building, but I will miss the stop-off in Craughwell where on enquiring if the apple tart was hot or cold, I was told, 'No. It's warm'.

There are some small villages which cannot be bypassed, such as Tarmonbarry in Longford because the bridge which spans the River Shannon is located in the centre of the village. Tarmonbarry is just a few short miles from Flancare Park, home to Longford Town football club, and known locally as 'The Flan Siro'! It's situated about three miles outside Longford town, on the Strokestown road.

We always seem to be in Flancare Park in the depths of winter and on bitterly cold nights, so it's good to have Keenan's in Tarmonbarry so close to hand. Good food, fast service, which is vital in our case, in and out in 40 minutes and ready to face the Arctic wind which forever seems to blow in Flancare Park. League of Ireland nights in Dalymount Park are in stark contrast to Flancare. Substitute Keenan's of Tarmonbarry with Eddie Rockett's in Phibsboro. The burgers are great but it's not quite the same.

There's a roadside diner, the Sperrin, outside Omagh, and it's a good stopping point on the way to the Brandywell or Ballybofey. A group of us ordered food there one afternoon a few years ago. The smoking ban had just been introduced in the Republic, and a number of the group went outside for a smoke while the food was being cooked. The day was wet, and the good man behind the bar noticed the gathering outside the door. He went out to them and said, 'Don't know why yez are all gettin' wet out here. Yez are in England now, and yez can smoke inside.'

Tricks of the Trade

To my eternal shame, there were times when we were mischievous on the road. For many years, *Know Your Sport* was a hugely popular sport quiz hosted by George Hamilton and Jimmy Magee. Four contestants appeared on each programme and their knowledge of sport was quite staggering as they battled to reach the grand final, where the winner received an Opel car presented by the genial Arnold O'Byrne from Opel Ireland.

Two programmes were recorded on the same night in the Donnybrook studios, one for the current week and the second to be transmitted a week later. The programme had a huge audience, and at 7.30 on Monday evenings every pub in Ireland was tuned in. We chancers would sit with the locals to watch a programme which we had worked on the previous week and, of course, knew who the winner was.

We were able to suggest that maybe the third contestant from the right was a 'sure thing', as we had seen him in a previous round.

But we came into our own in the 'mystery guest' round. This round was a very popular one, as Jimmy offered the contestants four clues as to the identity of the mystery guest, who was a well-known sporting personality, concealed behind the set. Four points were awarded to any contestant who could identify the guest after hearing the first clue, provided he could hit the buzzer before his rivals. The points decreased in value if the contestants failed to name the man or woman behind the screen.

A few of us were in a certain hostelry in the south one evening when Jimmy gave his first clue. The clue was 'four-four-two', and we shouted out the mystery man's name instantly: Eamon Coughlan – he wore singlet number 442 when he became world champion. The locals were mightily impressed. The final round was a quick-fire round, and we answered some of George's questions almost as quickly as he could ask them. We really made a huge impression on everyone. On that particular programme, one of the contestants correctly identified Eamon Coughlan after hearing the first clue. That's how high the standard was. Let me hasten to add that we admitted our guilt in the pub and confessed to having the inside track with regard to the questions. We did this because we knew that if we were discovered, we would probably have been run out of the place and rightly so.

One big fear we had before recording *Know Your Sport* was that the identity of the mystery guest would be known in advance. Before each recording, I had to do a final check around the main television reception to make sure that there were no stragglers from the audience still lurking about in the hope that they might spot the guest arriving. Producer Michael O'Carroll would meet up with the guest in a nearby hotel. It was only when we went into record mode that Mary Hogan, the driving force on *Know Your Sport*, would phone Michael to tell him the coast was clear. I had a major scare one evening prior to a recording.

As the audience made their way into the studio, I noticed Billy Morgan, former Cork captain and manager, wandering in with friends and families of the contestants. In panic, I bundled him out of the studio and asked him how he had managed to get that far. Billy was stunned, to put it mildly, and explained that he just came to Dublin to support one of his clubmates, who was a contestant that night. My enthusiasm had got the better of me. The mystery guest that night was Billy Coleman, the well-known rally driver from Cork, and quite similar to Morgan in looks. Billy Morgan has reminded me of that incident many times since.

After years of travelling the back roads of Ireland, many new friendships were forged all over the country. Pat Coakley introduced me to the Joe Costelloe golf classic which takes place in Galway each year, and of which he is the president. The event raise funds for Cancer Care West, and I have been delighted to help out in a small way over the last number of years.

Coakley's enthusiasm knows no bounds. Through his friends in Anfield and beyond he manages to assemble a Who's Who each year for the charity day. Liverpool legends Alan Hansen, Kenny Dalglish, Phil Neal, Ronnie Whelan, Jim Beglin and Gary Gillespie all return, year after year, and are delighted to give their time to a worthy cause. Former Evertonian and Irish international Kevin Sheedy is another regular. Gareth Edwards and Gerald Davies have both answered Coakley's call on a number of occasions and were able to meet up with former Irish internationals Mick Quinn and Moss Keane.

Craig Bellamy, who was playing for Liverpool at the time, proved how great Pat's power of persuasion was a few years ago. He had promised to come to Galway but missed his flight out of Cardiff. A car was waiting at Galway airport to pick him up from his Aer Arann flight from Dublin, but Bellamy was not on the flight. Undaunted by missing his flight, Bellamy hired a plane and a pilot to fly him directly to Galway. He had given his word that he would be there. The Joe Costelloe golf classic is a wonderful event and is run by a dedicated group of wonderful people. Since my own illness, it affords me an opportunity to help out, even in a small way, Cancer Care West.

I have been involved in sports coverage for over 40 years now, and I can safely say that I have enjoyed every minute of it. There were freezing cold wet and windy days and nights when I wondered about the sanity of being on a sideline in such conditions. Surely it would make more sense to be back in Donnybrook in a nice warm studio, instead of getting saturated in Thomond Park or Ballybofey or frozen in Athlone. But there's a buzz to be got from it. I have often asked myself where would I be if I were not working on a particular match. I would be watching it on television or I would be at the game. I will miss it when it comes to an end, and I got some advice a few months ago as to when that might be. Walking down the sideline in Tolka Park a gentleman in the crowd called me over.

'Hey RTÉ, c'mere!'

I went over to hear what he had to say, and he offered the following advice.

'Ye know what I'm goin to tell ya. You're comin' here since Adam and Eve and it's about fuckin' time ya packed it in!'

Maybe he's right.

On page 13 I mentioned the scenario posed by snooker referee John Williams and promised I would give you the answer. Here goes: If a player pots a red, fails to score with his next shot and still manages to make a break of 100, this is how it could happen.

Having potted the red, the player found himself snookered on all the colours. He nominated the pink ball but failed to hit it, giving six points away in the process. His opponent asked him to play the shot again, as was his right. At the second attempt, the player not only hit the pink ball but potted it too. It was a complete fluke. He then carried on to make a break of 100. Simple as that!

Bainisteoir

The 10 Greatest GAA Managers

Finbarr McCarthy

Bainisteoir tells the individual heroic stories of the GAA's 10 most successful managers – based on personal interviews given to the author.

- **Dublin's** Kevin Heffernan – how he trained the Dubs' teams for victory.
- **Kerry's** Mick O'Dwyer – the secrets of his long run of success with the Kingdom – and **Kildare**, **Laois** and **Wicklow**.
- **Kilkenny's** Brian Cody –the 4-in-a-row, his research, 'player management' and training routines.
- **Cork's** Billy Morgan – dogged by controversy and his outspoken nature – yet **he** achieved great things down South.
- **Meath's** Seán Boylan – how he combined an outstanding run of success with the 'royal' county and his role of 'Healer'.
- **Clare's** Ger Loughnane – followed by controversy at both Clare and **Galway** but he's a great motivator and retains the will to win.
- **Tyrone's** Mickey Harte – outsmarted Kerry and motivated his players to success.
- **Kerry's** Páidí Ó Sé – straight-talking stewardship of the Kingdom, and later with **Westmeath** and then . . . **Clare**.
- **Cork's** Jimmy Barry Murphy – hurling success on Leeside with an Adidas controversy and Greyhound-racing hobby.
- **Armagh's** Joe Kernan – how he achieved three-in-a-row in the Ulster Championship.

Working On A Dream

A year on the road with Waterford footballers

DAMIAN LAWLOR

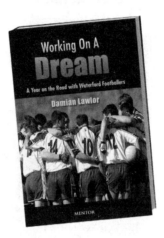

Far from the madding crowds of Croke Park, the inflated egos of star players and boardroom wrangles in the top counties, some GAA teams are fighting for their very existence....

Working On A Dream goes where no Irish sports book has ever gone before - a no holds barred, behind-the-scenes look at an intercounty GAA team struggling to survive at the lower end of the scale: Waterford senior footballers.

With access to all areas, the author, award-winning journalist Damian Lawlor, spent the 2009 season on trains, planes and in the dressing room with the Waterford players as they chase their goals for the year: climbing out of Division 4 of the national league and winning a championship game.

The tale that emerged is an honest, dramatic, sometimes tragic, sometimes comic depiction of what it's really like to be involved at the very grassroots of the GAA.

The Dark Side of Celebrity

Irish Courtroom Scandals of the Rich and Famous

LIAM COLLINS

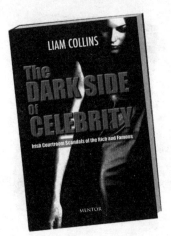

A journey to the other side of fame – telling the story of Ireland's rich and famous fighting each other across the courtroom floor. The stories of the sexual affairs, the alcohol abuse, the dirty tricks and the greed that ruined relationships and tore friendships apart.

- The beauty queen Michelle Rocca's bitter courtroom battle with Ryanair heir Cathal Ryan over a brawl at a socialite's birthday party.
- Solicitor-to-the-stars Elio Malocco and his dodgy dealings – leading to a falling out with Twink, the de Valera familly and the entire Law Society!
- How Manchester United boss Sir Alex Ferguson fell out with his Irish friend John Magnier over the wonder horse Rock of Gibraltar.
- How the sex of Bono's baby became a central issue in a court case that had absolutely nothing to do with him or U2.
- The Illusionist Paul Goldin disappears from a theatre stage and turns up in Hawaii with 'the other woman'.

Irish Family Feuds

Battles over Money, Sex and Power

LIAM COLLINS

When families fall out, the bitterness that emerges is matched only by the ferocity of their attacks on each other. Family feuds are far more vicious than disputes between strangers, as family members compete to crush each other completely and without mercy.

Cases include many rich and famous Irish families:

- Ben v Margaret – Duel at Dunnes
- The PV Doyle family 'hotel' war
- Comans and the 'Pub brawl'
- Enya, Clannad and the Brennan family feud
- 'Volkswagon vendetta' – the O'Flahertys' family secret

and many more family feuds over money, power and sex.

Larry Cunningham

A Showband Legend

Tom Gilmore

Despite a number of heart attacks, a cancer scare and several attempts at retirement, showband legend Larry Cunningham is still singing in his 70s. His story is a *potpourri* of humour, success, shady deals – as well as sadness, death and murder on the music scene.

Larry Cunningham was the first Irish artist to make the UK Pop Charts – long before U2, the Boomtown Rats, Boyzone or Westlife. His 'Tribute to Jim Reeves' spent over three months in the British hit parade, sold more than a quarter of a million copies and culminated in his appearance on *Top of the Pops* alongside Cliff Richard and others.

When 'Gentleman Jim' Reeves walked off the stage at a dance in Donegal, Larry's singing of Reeves' songs stopped an angry mob from burning the place down. His first No. 1 'Lovely Leitrim' sold over a quarter of a million but the song has sad links to a bloody shooting in a New York bar. The gunfight and deaths, as well as two forgotten song verses, are recalled in this book.

Fascinating reading for those interested in Showbands and Sixties nostalgia, Country 'n' Irish music, the rise and decline of the Ballroom dances and Jimmy Magee GAA All-Stars Football charity.